Praise for Was ‖‖‖‖‖‖‖ D1636845 / Bar Fighting:

"This book preaches what everyone should practice: diffuse when you can, subdue and control when you must. Finish the confrontation quickly and ferociously. These are lessons I have always taught, and these are the lessons found throughout *Bar-jutsu: The American Art of Bar Fighting*. It is a wonderfully presented approach to handling yourself in very real confrontational situations."

—Ed Martin, 15th Dan Shihan

"In the ring, I know my opponent and am prepared for combat. But outside the ring, things are less controlled. That's why I find *Bar-jutsu: The American Art of Bar Fighting* such an effective book. It provides very real scenarios, and very PRACTICAL ways of handling yourself when things are unpredictable. We're not talking dojos and judged competitions here, we're talking bars and drunken jerks. This book will quickly teach you how to be prepared and to know your opponent, even during chaos."

—Rod Salka, professional boxer, WBA NABA USA champion

"I wish everyone who walked into my bar had a little sensei in their head telling them what to do before a confrontation starts. That's exactly what this book does. It teaches in a very clear manner how to diffuse trouble before it starts, and how to end it before it escalates out of control."

—Pete Sparico, bar bouncer, Pittsburgh PA

"This book manages to make self-defense funny. From the very first pages it sets the tone; you can learn to defend yourself without being a stone-faced ninja. It is both an entertaining read and a practical guide for learning self-defense basics. Laugh and learn!" —Brad Sommer, Sommer Entertainment Group

"Bar-jutsu is much more than self-defense. In *Bar-jutsu: The American Art of Bar Fighting*, you get a total approach to conflict management. You'll learn how to diffuse trouble before it starts, how to carry yourself in a rowdy environment... and how to drop someone to their knees if they do happen to start trouble with you. The lessons are perfect for those of us not interested in becoming martial arts experts. If you want to feel more confident the next time you are in a crowded bar or other rowdy place, you really need to read this book."

—Mike Blade, professional wrestler

Published by Tuttle Publishing, an imprint of Periplus Editions (HK) Ltd.

www.tuttlepublishing.com

Copyright © 2013 James Porco and John Monaco

Bar-jutsu logo by James Porco and David Bissel

All original photographs by Brandon Kurta

All original artwork by Vincent Valerio

All rights reserved. No part of this publication may be reproduced or utilized in any form or by any means, electronic or mechanical, including photocopying, recording, or by any information storage and retrieval system, without prior written permission from the publisher.

Library of Congress Cataloging-in-Publication Data

Porco, James.
  Bar-jutsu : the American art of bar fighting / James Porco and John A. Monaco.
     pages cm
  ISBN 978-0-8048-4330-0 (pbk.)
  1. Ninjutsu. 2. Self-defense. I. Title.
  GV1114.73.P67 2013
  796.8--dc23
              2013016972

ISBN 978-0-8048-4330-0

First edition
16 15 14 13   5 4 3 2 1   1310CP

Distributed by

North America, Latin America & Europe
Tuttle Publishing
364 Innovation Drive, North Clarendon
VT 05759-9436 U.S.A.
Tel: 1 (802) 773-8930; Fax: 1 (802) 773-6993
info@tuttlepublishing.com
www.tuttlepublishing.com

Japan
Tuttle Publishing
Yaekari Building, 3rd Floor, 5-4-12 Osaki
Shinagawa-ku, Tokyo 141 0032
Tel: (81) 3 5437-0171; Fax: (81) 3 5437-0755
sales@tuttle.co.jp
www.tuttle.co.jp

Asia Pacific
Berkeley Books Pte. Ltd.
61 Tai Seng Avenue #02-12
Singapore 534167
Tel: (65) 6280-1330; Fax: (65) 6280-6290
inquiries@periplus.com.sg
www.periplus.com

Indonesia
PT Java Books Indonesia
Jl. Rawa Gelam IV No. 9
Kawasan Industri Pulogadung
Jakarta 13930, Indonesia
Tel: 62 (21) 4682 1088; Fax: 62 (21) 461 0206
crm@periplus.co.id
www.periplus.com

Printed in Singapore

TUTTLE PUBLISHING® is a registered trademark of Tuttle Publishing, a division of Periplus Editions (HK) Ltd.

BAR-JUTSU

★ The American Art ★
of Bar Fighting

JAMES PORCO
with JOHN MONACO

TUTTLE Publishing

Tokyo | Rutland, Vermont | Singapore

This book is dedicated to Ena and Molly.

BAR-JUTSU MENU

FOREWORD

I know we just met, but I already like you.

For one, you're the type of person that reads Forewords. That fact alone makes me want to buy you a drink.

And I'm guessing that a drink or two is just the sort of thing that you like. Just a hunch, but I see you as the type that enjoys an occasional visit to a bar. You probably have some interest in the martial arts or self-defense too. Or at least you have some interest in defending your collective body parts from harm. And you've just proven that you're the type that will pick up a book to learn a little more about how to do this.

I find all of these traits of yours commendable. You're OK in my book (that's a really bad pun, but you might as well get used to them—you'll find a few more before you reach the end of this book).

Of course, the practice of martial arts and the practice of bar-hopping may seem like polar opposites of the recreation spectrum. One involves discipline and control; the other, wings and beer. It's hard to imagine this odd couple cohabitating under the same book cover.

And yet, we've all been in a situation where a little discipline and control could have helped bring order to chaos. Enter *Bar-jutsu*. Not exactly a martial art, Bar-jutsu is more of an approach—a way of managing your behavior in potentially confrontational situations. And if there is one thing that bars serve up more than food and drinks, it's the potential for confrontation.

Simply put, Bar-jutsu is an approach that promotes the idea of having fun while staying safely and calmly in control. Bar-jutsu believes that a little preparedness and the right attitude toward self-defense go a long way toward letting the good times roll. It does not promote fighting or any form of aggression. Bar-jutsu is a belief in peaceful conflict resolution. It holds that most public confrontations can be resolved through an ability to remain calm...and to *laugh*. Its and old cliché, but laughter really is good medicine. And it doesn't leave a funny aftertaste.

Of course, Bar-jutsu also believes in physical maneuvers when needed—as long as they are employed to **defend only**. Should you ever encounter an aggressor who does not agree with your views on peace and humor, then you should be well-equipped to defend yourself and to subdue just long enough for the authorities to take control.

Bar-jutsu is a popular movement that already has a growing legion of fans. A number of bars have enthusiastically embraced it and are promoting Bar-jutsu activities. To ice the cake, there is even a team of lovely assistants—*The Bar-jutsu Girls*—to help promote the cause. You'll meet some of them throughout this book.

Bar-jutsu is the brainchild of James Porco, who first discussed the idea with me a few years ago. In many ways, Jim is the embodiment of Bar-jutsu; a fun guy that takes self-defense seriously. Jim has practiced defense and control on a daily basis for most of his professional career. He is an experienced and certified ninjutsu instructor. He has also been a professional wrestler (Van Hughes was the name back then). And for many years, he worked at a variety of bars as a bouncer. He has seen countless bar fights. In fact, he has enough stories to fill a book.

See where I'm going with this? But while a book full of stories about brawls would be plenty interesting on its own merit, Jim wanted more. He wanted to share lessons learned. He wanted to promote an idea; an approach. He wanted to combine the art, science, and technique of self-defense with the good, bad, and ugly that accompanies partying. He wanted something that would be a fun approach to a serious topic.

That approach would become Bar-jutsu. And now the movement has given birth to its first book, *Bar-jutsu: The American*

Art of Bar Fighting. He's a cute baby, isn't he? You can even take him along when you travel. He never cries on airplanes.

This book compiles advice from Jim and a variety of other professionals from fields such as law enforcement, martial arts, wrestling, and self-defense. It provides tips and techniques for managing very real, very confrontational situations that can typically occur in an environment such as a bar. Or a party. Or a wedding. Or the family reunion when someone calling himself "Uncle Auggie" shows up looking for a free drink.

Using step-by-step instructions, real and hypothetical scenarios, and graphic illustrations, *Bar-jutsu: The American Art of Bar Fighting* offers self-defense techniques designed to defend, subdue, and control. The techniques presented here are intended to be of use to those experienced in the martial arts, as well as those possessing basic self-defense training. But the easy-to-follow manner in which the maneuvers are presented make them just as helpful to novices, or to those who think "self-defense" means representing yourself in traffic court.

People for example, like me. I am a lover, not a fighter. In fact, I'm not even a lover. I'm a writer. I am as likely to start a fight as Ernest Hemingway or Edgar Allan Poe. Which is really saying something, because those guys are dead.

However, I am a big fan of bars and pubs. These places bring people from all walks of life together under one roof for laughs and camaraderie. Too often, we attach the idea of going to a bar to the idea of going somewhere to get drunk enough to forget what a jerk our boss is, or what our ex has just done to us. That's a sad injustice. Bars and pubs actually have a rich tradition. These places really do hold a significant place in the history of our social culture. But like many other things that are designed for good, bars are often abused. As much as I love them, I hate that they sometimes become places that offer the potential for trouble.

That is why I embrace the ideas of Bar-jutsu and of this book. I have witnessed firsthand how the Bar-jutsu approach lessens the potential for ugliness, even for someone like me. You won't become a master practitioner of ninjutsu or any other formal martial art. But you may not be looking for that. If you're like me, you may simply be looking for a few tips to help ensure the night out will be the good time you planned for when you left the house.

Bar-jutsu: The American Art of Bar Fighting is an educational, realistic, and humorous introduction to self-defense training for a specialized environment. With a little practice, readers can easily master each of the techniques presented, providing a basic set of self-defense maneuvers perfectly-suited for diffusing bar scuffles.

So sit back and enjoy. Read the lessons. Practice the maneuvers. Stare at the Bar-jutsu Girls. Practice the maneuvers again. Then go to your favorite bar and…do nothing. Simply enjoy yourself. Do not behave as though you have somehow just transformed yourself into "Bar-jutsu Man: Defender of the People." However, should trouble find you, recall the lessons of this book and do your best to resolve, defend, subdue, control, and cooperate with authorities.

I hope to see you at the bar soon. If I do, don't let me forget that I owe you a drink, you forward-thinking, Foreword-reading fanatic.

John A. Monaco
Freelance writer and lover of bars,
clubs, pubs, taverns, and saloons

INTRODUCTION

As a species, mankind should be a reasonably proud bunch. We've grown from cave-dwelling hunters and gatherers, to penthouse-dwelling patrons of five-star restaurants. We've learned to walk upright, ride on wheels, and even fly. We've survived dinosaurs, plagues, disco, and infomercials. We gazed at the stars in awe, and then we found a way to reach them.

We may no longer live in caves, but we still share a few things with our Neanderthal ancestors. The stars still come out at night. And when they do, we still like to gather beneath them. We come together to break bread, look for mates, and tell stories. But what once occurred around the glow of a fire now unfolds by the glow of neon bar lights.

Ah yes, the bar. Quite possibly the single-greatest advancement in socialization. A place to unwind. To watch a game. A place to meet, greet, and eat. And of course, a place to drink. Because somewhere between learning to make fire and learning to make firearms, we learned to make firewater. And when you add alcohol to the mix, some of us can act, well...like Neanderthals. We get territorial. We thump our chests. We see something (or someone) we like, and we go on the hunt. Sometimes we'll even fight each other for dominance. That's when a bar becomes more than a great place to have fun. It becomes a great place to receive some unexpected dental work. A little self-defense can go a long way to help the civilized defend themselves from those who are channeling their inner-caveman.

That's where this book comes in. *Bar-jutsu: The American Art of Bar Fighting* provides basic tips that can help you the *very next time* your night out is interrupted by a troublemaking troglodyte who is bent on setting mankind back a few million years. Nothing in this book is intended to make you a master of any martial art or self-defense discipline. But by sharing our thoughts on confrontational public situations, and by providing examples of a few fundamental defensive maneuvers, we believe you will be better equipped to resolve a confrontation while protecting yourself and your guests.

Bar-jutsu does NOT promote bar fighting. In fact, we resoundingly oppose it. We love bars...and parties, and anyplace where a good time is happening. Fighting does more than ruin faces. It ruins fun. We don't take kindly to someone ruining fun. It's like sucker-punching Santa Claus.

Bars have a great history. From the small town pubs of ancient Europe, to the taverns of colonial America, to the saloons of the old wild West, bars have always been about coming together for laughs, food, and drinks. The very same things that our prehistoric ancestors used to love doing after a big hunt. Sure, we've since modified the menu to replace freshly-killed buffalo with buffalo wings, but the basic idea remains.

We have visited bars across the county and have found that many are like family to their community, right down to the proudly hung pictures of customers found on the walls. Business deals are made in bars. Lifelong friends are made in bars. People even meet their future mates in bars. Bars are like social media, without the media to embarrass you the next morning.

So we take offense to those who bring violence into these places that we have come to love and appreciate so much. Of course, we're not blind to the bad that sometimes happens there. But don't blame the bar for the bums that walk in. They can card to keep the under-aged out, but there is no card to identify jerks. Inevitably, one or two Cro-Magnon maniacs are going to make their way in, eager to give a more ancient meaning to the term "clubbing."

While training with Shihan Ed Martin (better known as "Papasan"), we picked up an interesting quote. He often said "Don't play with your food. This person attacked you; he isn't the top of the food chain." Aggressors in a bar aren't worth much effort in our minds. So we're all in favor of doing whatever is necessary to subdue them, and then letting someone else get them out of the place. The less energy wasted, the better. The less violence in one of our favorite places, the better.

We have seen enough bar fights to know that they are not the pretty affairs that Hollywood portrays. In the movies, bar fights are often comical scenes. The hero—despite being restrained by two goons—sends an attacker sailing over the bar with a single punch. Then, for no apparent reason, two other patrons look at each other, say something profound like "Why not?" and start swinging as well. Someone playfully smashes a bottle over someone else's head, and soon a room full of stuntmen join the fracas. Within minutes you have a complete melee, all set to the tune of some really awful 1980s song or honky-tonk piano solo.

Real life, of course, gets much uglier than this. People get hurt, sometimes seriously. Bouncers get involved. Police show up. A combatant of a bar fight is rarely treated like some hero afterward, getting slaps on the back for "teaching those guys a lesson." If you are lucky enough to make it home afterward, it is usually with the help of a friend. But more often, you first take a detour to an emergency room. Or a jail cell.

The Bar-jutsu Basics

By now a few things should be clear. We like fun. We hate fighting. Bar-jutsu promotes the idea of having all the fun with none of the fighting. And when necessary, you should be able to appropriately defend yourself, subduing aggressors until authorities can restore order.

For these reasons we have identified four fairly obvious yet really important things that we like to bring up whenever we have the opportunity. And since this is our book, we think now is a great opportunity:

- **Fairly obvious yet really important thing #1:** *Fighting is Really Stupid*

Bar-jutsu is all about having fun; enjoying yourself wherever your social calendar happens to place you for the evening. Fighting is the very opposite of this. Fighting not only presents a danger to you, to your guests, and to innocent bystanders. It also destroys the fun for everyone. We believe that there is nothing quite as prehistoric as two people striking each other in anger. Millions of years of human development should have taught us better than this. If fighting is something you find enjoyable, we suggest that you avoid bars and instead make your way to a place where your favorite pastime is welcome. Like the set of an afternoon syndicated talk show. Or among a wedding crowd as the bride throws her bouquet.

- **Fairly obvious yet really important thing #2:** *Fighting Is Not Self-defense*

The term "self-defense" comes from the ancient Latin term "defendamus mea ass," which translates as "if you touch-a this toga, I break-a u face." OK, that's not exactly true. But even the ancients knew that self-defense is a simple concept that is just what the name implies...DEFENSE of ONESELF. Defense is only needed if there is a real threat. People may laugh at your dance moves, heckle your karaoke singing, or even call you out for wearing white pants. None of these things are threats. None of these things require you to retaliate physically. In fact, if you retaliate physically against someone who is verbally assaulting you, then all you have done is start a fight. Only when someone else makes a purposeful, aggressive, physical move should you ever consider physical defense.

That being said...please get rid of those white pants.

- **Fairly obvious yet really important thing #3:** *To Avoid Fighting, Avoid a Fight*

Bar-jutsu is a belief in resolving confrontational situations in the most peaceful means possible. Sometimes this is matter of placing yourself in the right place at the right time. Or removing yourself from the wrong place at just the right time. Confrontations can very often be diffused verbally. Choice of words is important. Avoid "hot" words that instigate fights. It may be a simple matter of offering to buy the confrontational caveman a drink.

Humor is great for lightening the mood and cooling hot heads. Ever try to pummel someone who is wielding a rubber chicken? OK probably not. But if you did, you'd find that it's really difficult.

- **Fairly obvious yet really important thing #4:** *Attackers Attack, and Defenders Defend*

Despite your best efforts, your attacker may be sold on the idea of turning your verbal confrontation to a physical one. You will know this because the attacker will attack. He will make the first move. That is what attackers do. That is NOT what defenders do. Defenders defend. They ready themselves. They remain prepared and cautious. As a defender, you should NEVER be the first to strike or to make any sort of physical contact with the other party. Nor should you ever agree to take an argument outside. Or rip your shirt off and encourage your opponent with testosterone-induced chants like "Let's go tough guy...I'm right here." We especially ask that you keep that shirt on if you have just eaten the "Belly Buster Special."

At some point a potential attacker—particularly an intoxicated one—may attack. He may make that very first move that changes the game from "Charades" to "Twister," taking the confrontation from a verbal one to a physical one. The maneuvers presented in this book are designed to help you respond appropriately to these types of actions.

These four principles are what Bar-jutsu represents. It is a movement promoting fun, restraint, resolution, and control. In *Bar-jutsu: The American Art of Bar Fighting*, we identify ways to take control of situations in bars and similar places before they get out of hand. We promote the notion of resolving confrontations without resorting to violence. And we demonstrate ways to control attackers who resort to violence themselves.

Your night out is all about a good time. A little restraint can help a verbal confrontation from becoming a physical one. And proper defense technique can help you to handle those who cross the line, maintaining some control until authorities take over. And recent studies suggest that over 95% of all smoking-hot women prefer a man who controls a bar scuffle and walks away unscathed over one who loses his front teeth and is escorted out in handcuffs.

But Wait! Read Now and We'll Also Include...

Many of the maneuvers presented in this book are based on the martial art of *ninjutsu*. Bar-jutsu draws on the experience of certified ninjutsu practitioners and trainers, as well as other martial art practitioners, bar bouncers, law enforcement agents, and even professional wrestlers. (Note: *Bar-justu* does NOT condone hitting your opponent with a folding chair.) This collection of experience will help to "connect the dots" between martial arts theory and social situations that could benefit from disciplined methods of gaining control. This book will help you to identify those situations, and to act appropriately to defend yourself.

As you read through this book, you'll find a number of bits and pieces that are designed to help the cause. These include:

- **Lessons** – *This book presents a variety of simple, basic maneuvers that can be quickly learned and mastered. Each maneuver is presented in a separate lesson, which includes an introduction, step-by-step tutorials, and images. Many of the images include the Bar-jutsu Girls. If you won't pay attention to us, perhaps you'll pay attention to them.*

- **Scenarios** – *Each lesson begins with a scenario. The scenarios are based on real events; something that we have actually witnessed or been a part of. Of course, we didn't really snap photos of altercations as they were happening. That would have just been weird. Instead, we've recreated them here with help from the Bar-jutsu Players, a group of folks we have brought together to help demonstrate a few things. Think of it as a little theatrical production, all for the benefit of your training.*

- *Bar-jutsu says* – *There is a good deal of material in this book. Personally, we find it all fascinating. But we understand if you do not take every word of it to memory. To help drive home the more important points, you will find an occasional call-out referred to as "Bar-jutsu says." Consider these wise pieces of advice from your Bar-jutsu sensei.*

- *Reality Bar-jutsu* – *Much like "reality TV," Reality Bar-jutsu will give you a taste of someone else's real life that you can enjoy from the comfort of your easy chair. The goal is to demonstrate how the lessons presented in this book have been utilized in true-life situations. At the very least, you can laugh at the antics of people acting foolishly, or cheer on your favorite combatants. With practice, you can use Bar-Jutsu to be a survivor instead of getting tossed off the island. And while we can't promise that you'll find yourself dancing with the stars, a little practice can help you to avoid seeing them after a brawl.*

Please take the time to read the following lessons **carefully**. Practice the moves properly, with a friend and in a safe environment. While we love to have fun with these topics, the reality is that the practice of self-defense maneuvers is nothing to play around with. Practice slowly at first, and take it seriously. No horseplay. Don't make us come down there.

We hope you enjoy the lessons and stories presented in this book. Happy training! As our club-wielding ancestors used to say... "GUBBA KA" (which, loosely translated, means "Cheers").

LESSON 1:
MAKING AN ENTRANCE

Bar-jutsu is all about defending yourself should a big night out bring a little unexpected trouble your way. It is a collection of tips, techniques, and general advice to keep you and your guests safe from injury. The techniques found throughout this book are simple to learn and easy to employ.

But let's cut to the chase. We really appreciate the fact that you've purchased this book. (You didn't steal it, did you?) So we'd like to offer you a special customer courtesy. Rather than ask you to read through the entire book before building up to some climactic finale, we would like to present to you—right out of the gate—the single-most POWERFUL technique we have ever learned. We are ready right here and now to present an ironclad method GUARANTEED to ensure that you will never have any trouble in a bar. Years of research and consultation with some of the best minds in the business make it possible to present to you the single most effective technique available. Never known to fail, it is guaranteed to separate you from any trouble, in any bar, anywhere.

The secret?

Never enter a bar. Or a club. Or a party.

OK, so perhaps our best technique is a little bent. You wouldn't be reading this if you wanted to avoid bars. We may have just met you, but we already know you better than that. So…now what?

Since your entrance is inevitable, it might as well be productive. When it comes to walking into a bar, making an entrance is about much more than being fashionably late in your finest polyester suit and gold chains. If done properly, you can actually make your entrance your very first line of defense.

Bar-jutsu says: When done properly, your entrance into any event that has the potential for confrontation (a bar, a party, etc.) becomes your first line of self-defense.

So This Guy Walks into a Bar…

Anytime you walk into a bar, you should make the time to absorb as much of your surroundings as possible. At the risk of sounding a little "zen," you really would do well to become one with your surroundings. Become completely aware of the atmosphere that you have just walked into. Absorb as much of your environment as you can.

This is not as easy or obvious as it may seem. Most of us process dozens of thoughts with our first few steps into a bar. Unfortunately self-defense usually doesn't make the list. Instead, our brain cells are busy with matters such as:

- *Is that girl checking me out?*
- *What's on tap?*

- *Is that girl a dude?*
- *Is it still happy hour?*
- *Is that dude-girl checking me out?*

Who are we to argue with your brain cells? But securing your safety is what this lesson is all about. So it may first be better to consider the following:

- *Where are the exits?*
- *Are there potential makeshift weapons (like pool sticks or darts) to watch out for?*
- *Does it seem particularly rowdy tonight?*
- *Are there noisy groups congregating in various sections of the place?*
- *Do I see anyone that I know? Are they friends? They're not ex-girlfriends are they? Oh no...Is that Rachel? Oh $@#&!*

Little things like this may not seem immediately important. However, these are the very types of details that can make a difference should things get uglier than your Great-Aunt Agnes. A survey of your surroundings is a spoonful of preventative medicine that can help spare you from waking up with more than just a hangover to heal from.

If you've ever traveled on an airplane, you are familiar with the brief pre-takeoff safety presentation. But be honest...unless the flight attendant is Sonya the September Centerfold, you're completely ignoring her as she points out the emergency exits, aren't you? However, what if that plane found itself in an emergency situation...say, slowly sinking into the Atlantic? If you needed to get out quickly, you would likely find yourself wishing that you'd paid attention to more than Sonya's own personal flotation devices.

Similarly you will want to make sure that IF a fight begins, you can quickly navigate to an exit. There is nothing wrong with heading for the doors if a fight breaks out. It is no more cowardly than making your way to the emergency exit on that sinking airplane.

Remember, you walked into this place looking for a fun time; walking out is just your way of staying on task.

That is not to say that you should walk into a bar *expecting* a fight to break out. But you should certainly be prepared for the unexpected. There is a very real possibility that your evening will be trouble-free regardless. Just like there is a very real chance that your flight will take off and land without a hitch. But the *one time* when something *does* happen…preparedness becomes your best friend.

Preparedness only comes with familiarity. So after walking *into* the bar, simply *walk* the bar. Check out everything you can. Look for anything that someone may try to use as a weapon in the heat of battle. Get a feel for things like the floor. Can you establish proper footing, or is it covered in beer (or a mystery fluid that you really hope is only beer)?

Walking the bar can also help you get a feel for who is in there. Covertly listen to conversations. Try to determine who has already had too much to drink. Observe everything that you can, but do not be an instigator.

The biggest x-factor here is alcohol. You simply can never know with any certainty what a night of drinking will do to someone who is celebrating, or trying to forget a bad day, or trying to break a Jagermeister record. Some bar patrons drink and become lambs. Others drink and become lions. Still others drink and become crazed butcher-knife-wielding circus clowns (or at least that is what happens in our dreams after eating late-night tacos).

The single-best defense against unpredictability is preparedness. Be prepared for any realistic scenario. It is almost a guarantee that any troublemaker you encounter will not be prepared. So you will already have an advantage. By treating your entrance like a line of defense, by surveying your surroundings, and by be-

Bar-jutsu says: The single-best defense against unpredictability is preparedness. It gives you an immediate and significant advantage over your opponent.

ing prepared, you already have a very real competitive advantage over anyone who may present a threat. And this is *before* any physical contact is made. It's like winning a round of a boxing match before the opening bell.

Of course, the alternative is to completely avoid the bar. Staying out of the place significantly increases your chances of avoiding a bar scuffle. And you can use the free time to catch up with your Great-Aunt Agnes. What could possibly go wrong there?

Lesson 2:

FIRST CONTACT: HEY! HE TOUCHED ME

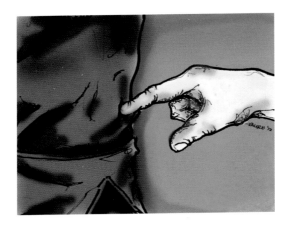

We'd like to spend the next two lessons getting a little touchy feely with you. But don't worry, we're not going to ask you to open up and talk about your feelings. Nobody here wants that.

No, we're referring to literally touchy. And literally feely.

There are countless reasons that bar altercations begin. Sometimes it's over a woman. OK, *many times* it's over a woman. But it can just as easily happen over sports. Or a joke gone wrong. Often two people who have some bad history end up running into each other. We've even seen a few fights erupt over politics (can full-contact political debates really be far behind?). The reality is, when you pack a large crowd into a confined area where alcohol is being served, almost anything can be the spark that ignites a fire.

But of all the reasons for scuffles, the one that we have most frequently observed is what we call "first contact"...that moment when someone first makes physical contact with someone else. It doesn't matter if it was accidental or incidental. Very often, just reaching out to touch someone is an invitation to the fight club.

While things may seem to move in slow motion when you've had too much to drink, most incidents of first contact actually occur in the blink of an eye. And just that quickly, you must determine if the contact was an accident or an act of aggression.

Unless you are very certain that the contact was accidental, the best approach is to assume it was not. The actual level of aggression is not important at this point. If someone has demonstrated a willingness to purposefully invade your personal space once—even incidentally—you must assume they are willing to do so again. And what started as something incidental could soon escalate to something aggressive.

Bars are difficult places to avoid contact. In particularly crowded spots, it takes very little to get tempers flaring. Often it is difficult to determine what the intent of first contact is. A poke to the chest is easy to interpret. But something like a bump in passing is a little more complicated.

So how can you be 100% certain that the first contact is not an act of aggression? How do you know that you are not simply overreacting to a harmless incidental bump? How should you decide when it is time to go into self-defense mode?

We have developed a simple test for you to use. If you take the time to commit this to memory, you will be able to utilize this test on-site to evaluate the circumstances you find yourself in. It is simple, straightforward, and effective.

Here's how it works…simply compare your particular situation to the following two scenarios. If your situation more closely resembles Scenario (A), you can be assured you are safe; if your situation more closely resembles Scenario (B), you should remain on guard and prepared:

SCENARIO (A): You are standing in a bar with some friends. A sexy waitress spins around quickly after taking someone's order. She runs into you during her pirouette, accidentally falling into your arms. From there, she looks into your eyes and says "Oh my, now look at what you've done. You are so handsome and strong that I completely forgot the order I just took. Now I'm in trouble. I guess I am going to have to quit my job and run away with you."

SCENARIO (B): Wow. This is awkward. Uh, nothing close to Scenario (A) is ever going to happen to you. You belong here in (B). Sorry.

So the best approach is to assume that *any* first contact has the potential to be an aggressive move.

Remember: Bar-jutsu *does not* promote fighting. However, physical contact should immediately raise a red flag in your mind. From the very minute that you find yourself on the receiving end of first contact, you should be in self-defense mode. Unless you are 100% certain this contact was not purposeful, you should be on guard and prepared.

Bar-jutsu says: If someone makes first contact with you, be on high alert. Assume the potential for aggression, but never retaliate. Give the potential attacker an opportunity to prove intent first.

Step Back, Mouth...The Brain's Got This

Again, the single most important thing about first contact is to be on alert only. Never retaliate physically. Recall one of the Bar-jutsu basics we discussed in the Introduction of this book: *attackers attack and defenders defend*. First contact is a warning shot, not an act of war.

But once contact has been made, it is time for you to prepare. At this point, your mouth and your brain should be doing two very different things. Your mouth should take a time out. No need to encourage a potential attacker to do his thing by saying anything that will escalate a showdown. Remain calm. Remain cool. Remain polite. And just listen. Altercations never begin by listening too much. Who knows…maybe an apology is coming. Better yet, maybe an offer for a free drink is coming.

While your mouth is taking a break, your brain should be working overtime. Take in as much of the situation as you can. Does the potential attacker seem intoxicated? Is he alone? Is he holding anything that can be used as a weapon? Are there any clues that could suggest which side is his dominant side? (A wristwatch on the right arm, for example, may possibly suggest a left-handed opponent). Does his behavior seem odd or suggest that he is about to make any sort of move toward you?

It is VERY rare that first contact is actually the first blow of an altercation. At worst, it is usually the opening bell; the call for fighters to come out from their corners and stare each other down while a referee reminds them of the rules. If your mouth and brain have done their jobs, you can be assured that 1) you have done nothing to incite an attack and 2) you are prepared to defend should an attack come anyway.

Of course the first contact can ultimately lead to an attack. You will likely know when the attack comes. The intent of first contact is not always clear, but the actual attack usually is. Attackers are usually not subtle, they will make the attack clear and purposeful. And that is when the altercation becomes a physical one.

Bar-jutsu says: The very minute that an aggressor makes any sort of purposeful physical contact, the confrontation goes from being a verbal one to being a physical one.

Let's now look at a scenario in which you do everything right, but simply cannot avoid the aggression. It is a little like getting too close to the edge of a waterfall in a rowboat. At some point, no matter how much you row, you come to realize that you are going over the edge. Similarly, at some point you may come to realize that no matter how much you try to avoid it, a scuffle is about to happen. Someone is going to get touchy feely with you.

Setting the Scene: First Contact: Hey! He Touched Me

You are enjoying your evening in a bar (get used to this...most of our scenarios begin this way). You notice a girl seated at the opposite side of the bar, and decide to approach her and do that voodoo that you do so well. You make your way to her and offer to buy her a drink. She accepts and soon you are engaged in conversation.

Unfortunately, you have an audience. Someone is watching—and not enjoying the show. It seems that a guy across the room had earlier tried the very same thing with the very same girl. But with very different results. He failed miserably; your new friend showed no interest in him. In a perfect world, he'd be happy for you two, maybe even to the point of leaving to go pick out a nice toaster or other future wedding gift for you. But instead he's a little touchy, and is planning on getting a little feely. Act 1 of his play "You Should Have Picked Me Instead, You Evil Witch Woman" is about to begin.

Back at the front bar, you politely excuse yourself to go to the restroom (is it any wonder she's crazy about you?). On your way there, you are greeted by your adversary, who bumps into you. His manners, his facial expression, his poor aptitude for acting, even his breath...everything about the situation makes it obvious that this contact is no accident. Recalling your Bar-jutsu training, you remain calm. You smile and say something polite, like:

"Excuse me buddy. I'm just trying to get to the men's room."

But what he hears you say instead is something along the lines of:

> *"Excuse me butthead. Remember that girl at the bar that you could barely get a hello from? Well she's been clinging to me like that zit is clinging to your face. I'm about to take her home, where we will do things to each other that you can't even pronounce. I'm just trying to get to the men's room to freshen up first. Want me to say hi to your mom if I see her in there?"*

Needless to say, you are not getting past the troll without paying the toll. He makes an aggressive move toward you. Let's now take a look at one way that you might respond to a situation like this. Remember, we call this lesson "Hey He Touched Me" for a reason; you should not find yourself in this predicament unless an attacker purposefully and aggressively reaches out to touch you.

Introduction to the Maneuver:
First Contact: Hey! He Touched Me.

1. Recall that our aggressor's fall from grace began with his failed attempt to get the same interest from your new friend that you have.

2. As you step away from the bar to head to the rest room, you are greeted with a hello that is about as subtle as a hockey check against the boards.

3. Despite your efforts to diffuse, he makes the move. He places his hand on you in an aggressive manner that makes it very clear you now need to defend yourself. Adjust your body so that you are square with him.

4. Secure his hand firmly against you. This will destroy his balance and give you the opportunity to actually use his move to initiate your own. Apply as much pressure as necessary to hold his hand in place. He gave you that hand...it's yours now!

5. Bring your left hand up and trap his right hand against your body. Step back and to the left, pulling him forward, thus throwing his balance off.

6. Swap your left hand with your right hand, placing your right palm against the back of his hand and grabbing the meaty part of his hand between the wrist and pinky finger.

7. Once you grab his hand, use your body, not your arm, to roll his hand across your chest and to the right. This is done by turning your upper body back to the right. Now slide your left hand down to his elbow and push it inward, locking it and sliding your right foot back. Drive him to the ground. It is important to remember

to use your entire body to overpower his pushing arm. Do not "arm wrestle" him.

8. Keep his hand trapped on your body and do not release him. Applying the proper torque is also important. As you roll his arm, imagine taking his pinky knuckle and pushing it back towards him diagonally across his forearm. The purpose of this is to create strain on his arm. The pain he will feel will cause his entire body to give up and lean forward to attempt to reduce pressure.

PRACTICING THE MOVE:

1. Both partners stand at arm's length across from each other squared at the shoulders.

2. The attacker will push with the right hand against defenders left shoulder.

3. As the defender's left hand comes up to trap the pushing hand against his chest, defender will step back at a 45 degree angle on the same side as the pushing hand destroying the attacker's balance.

4. The defender's right hand will come across his body, grabbing the inside of the attacker's palm, placing the defender's right palm on the back of the attacker's hand.

5. As the defender rolls the hand across his own chest, he steps back with the right foot and turning the upper body to the right.

6. The left hand will now slide down to the elbow, locking it in place and applying pressure to drive the attacker in the desired direction.

7. Make sure to breathe and keep your back straight, never bending over, and using proper footwork to maintain your own balance.

8. Repeat steps for both right and left sides.

FIRST CONTACT: OOPS! I TOUCHED HIM

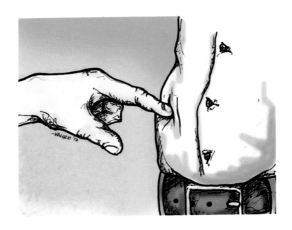

"Well Your Honor, I was sitting at the bar minding my own business, when this perpetrator fella reaches over to grab the beer he ordered. And then...and then..."

"I know this is difficult, sir. Just take your time."

"Thank you, Your Honor. Anyway, this guy reaches for his beer and then...he...well...bumps into me!

"Order...Order in the court! I'm sorry for the outburst. Please proceed".

"Anyway...he bumps me. He tries to say that he is all sorry and stuff, but...but...he bumped me! It all happened so quickly. It was so horrible, so senseless. All so that he could get that stupid beer of his. A...light beer."

"Order...I said order in the court! One more outburst and I will have this courtroom cleared. Now...tell us what happened next."

"I guess I sort of beat him with my bar stool and marinated him in his light beer".

"As well you should have. It is the opinion of this court that you acted in self-defense, and that your heroic behavior likely saved others from danger as well. You are free to go, and may time heal the emotional scars of your ordeal."

You're not likely to see a scene like this play out in a courtroom. But in a barroom, this kind of mentality makes itself right at home. For some people, alcohol only strengthens their belief in the sovereignty of their personal space. And they are quick to unleash their own personal army, navy, and air force to defend that sovereignty.

We have been in many bars where the entire place seemed to have a mood all its own. Some evenings the crowd seems happy and celebratory. Other times a bar can seem like an irritable mate who has just been insulted. On those nights, a simple accidental bump can be enough to unleash Hurricane "Oh-No-He-Didn't."

It should be no newsflash to you that bars can often get crowded. Certain areas—like the order stations or the restrooms or entry ways—can get especially congested. You would have to bob and weave like Keanu Reeves in *The Matrix* to avoid touching anyone.

In Lesson 2 we discussed some tips for handling confrontations that can occur when someone makes first contact with you. It is just as likely however that you are the one making first contact. An accidental bump while reaching for your beer is actually a mild example. An overzealous backslapper may cause you to spill that beer on someone else. The home team might score, sending your loaded nachos flying. What starts as a simple slip can cause a chain reaction that looks more like a multiple car pileup on the expressway. Road rage can be right around the corner.

In a courtroom, a judge or jury can sort the facts out. Somebody wins a verdict, somebody wins an orange jumpsuit. In the bar, the scales of justice tilt a little differently. The facts don't always matter. If someone suddenly finds that they are wearing your drink, it may not matter that it was an accident. What you consider a minor mistake can be viewed as the crime of the century. Or at least the crime of the evening.

If you find yourself the perpetrator of first contact, your first response is critical to making your case. As we discussed in Lesson Two, a confrontation can often be diffused verbally, and your first move should always be a conciliatory one. The victim's first reaction may very well be anger, and he may even retaliate with a minor push back. Do not interpret this as the first blow. This likely is only his own attempt at self-defense, better known as intimidation. Stay on guard, but do not escalate the matter.

Bar-jutsu says: A potential attacker only has the potential for attack. He may react to accidental contact with minor contact of his own, but this is not yet an attack. Do not relax, but do not retaliate physically.

Instead of returning shove with shove, there are a number of simple verbal responses you can attempt in order to diffuse. Similarly, there are a few things you should definitely avoid saying. Here are a few examples of each:

APPROPRIATE THINGS TO SAY AFTER ACCIDENTAL FIRST CONTACT:
- *"Hey dude, I'm really sorry. Are you OK?"*
- *"My bad. Let me buy you a new drink."*

INAPPROPRIATE THINGS TO SAY AFTER ACCIDENTAL FIRST CONTACT:
- *"Sorry for bumping into your girl. But at least now I know—they're definitely fake."*

- *"Actually you should be thanking me. That draft beer you're wearing now smells a lot better than your cologne. Probably costs more too."*

As we've noted several times already, most heated exchanges can be resolved peacefully. It's much like settling out of court; everybody wins. Your victim gets an apology and maybe even a free drink, while you get to avoid a fight. Most often these things can blow over quickly anyway, and what seems like a first-degree reason to fight one minute is a distant memory the next. We've seen many examples of people coming close to blows at happy hour only to act like lifelong friends by last call.

But just as we saw in Lesson 2, sometimes you will run into someone uninterested in your words. Despite throwing yourself on the mercy of the court, they may be determined to throw the book at you. And since you're in a bar, they'll be unlikely to find a book. That means you're getting something worse thrown at you, like a bar stool. Or a jukebox.

Let's take a look at another scenario. This time, you are the perpetrator of first contact. Don't feel too guilty: all you've done is bump someone while reaching for the beer you just ordered. But your victim has decided to give himself the title of judge, jury, and (especially) executioner. Fortunately you have the legal team of Bar-jutsu & Bar-jutsu behind you. OK, so technically we're not lawyers, but we passed a different kind of bar exam and we are prepared to help you defend your case. And your face.

Setting the Scene: First Contact: Oops! I Touched Him

You and your friends are seated at a table in a bar. It's a busy evening, and while there is a waitress assigned to your table you feel badly about how busy she is. So you decide to walk to the bar and order your next drink yourself. Actually it has more to do with you being thirsty and impatient. But we'll embellish a bit. It's our scenario and we want you to look good.

You squirm your way between some folks seated at the bar. One patron in particular is really unhappy about your squeeze play, and gives you a look that drives the point home.

Strrriiiike one.

On a dare from your friends you've been instructed to order the new "Barbie Beer," a hot pink-colored zero-calorie beer popular with the ladies. Most of the people overhearing you order this just laugh at you, but your new Siamese twin just shakes his head in disgust.

Strrriiiike two.

As the bartender hands you your "beer," you accidentally bump the guy.

Strrriiiike three.

Well, not exactly a strike. In his mind, it's more like you've just beaned him in the head with a fastball. He has no interest in quietly taking his base. He's charging the mound.

He rises from his barstool and immediately makes it known it isn't an act of respect. As usual, you make every attempt to resolve the issue peacefully. You apologize, and even offer to buy him a drink. In return, he grabs you by the shirt.

By now, you know what this means. The altercation is now a physical one. Let's look at a new maneuver that can be used to subdue your grumpy new adversary.

Introduction to the Maneuver: Oops! I Touched Him

1. You make your move for you drink, when something goes bump in the night. Sadly, the something is you. And your victim isn't afraid. In fact, by now he's had enough of you.

(Note: You may notice that the guy playing you looks an awful lot like the guy who just got his arm twisted in Lesson 2. Remember, the **Bar-jutsu Players** *are here to demonstrate a few things. They're flexible enough to play the villain in one lesson and the victim in the next.)*

2. You try all the Bar-jutsu best practices, but your apologies and offers for a drink mean nothing. He grabs your shirt. There is no going back now—you are in self-defense mode.

3. As your opponent grabs you, grab his right arm by the shirt-sleeve. Bring your right hand inside and grab his shirt at his left shoulder. Twist his body by pushing his left shoulder back and pulling his right arm toward you.

4. Once you have his upper body turned, release your right hand hold and reach for that beer. When his adrenaline has kicked in he will not let go of his hold on you, which is exactly what you want. Roll your right arm counter-clockwise and point your thumb downward. As you "reach for your beer," you shoot passed his shoulder and then bend your knees to lower your body. As  this happens, lock the crook of your elbow with the crook of his.

5. Roll his arm in by making a circular motion with your right arm and raise your body once again.

6. While your right hand is doing all of this work, you can release your left hand and drive your middle finger into his throat, applying pressure to his sternum, at the top where the collar bone meets in the center of the throat.

And if anyone asks you what happened...you were simply reaching for your beer.

PRACTICING THE MANEUVER

(For this technique make sure that both you and your partner are wearing shirts with sleeves. It is much easier to understand the move if you are grabbing articles of clothing.)

1. Both partners stand at arm's length away from each other squared at the shoulders.

2. Mirror each other by grabbing at the shoulder on the right and the elbow on the left.

3. Defender shall step back and to the left at 45 degrees while simultaneously pushing forward with the right hand (grabbing the shoulder) and pulling back on the left elbow. Allow attacker to take a step forward since his balance is now gone.

4. Defender will release hold of right hand and shoot past attacker, staying close to the body. Defender extends are out with palm facing away from attacker and thumb pointing down.

6. Bend your knees to lower your body while at the same time rotating right arm clockwise at the elbow. As you rotate arm and bring to center of chest raise your body to upright position. Attacker should maintain strong grip throughout technique until unable to hold on.

7. Release left hand and drive middle finger into the defender's sternum at the top where the collarbone meets. You can also join your hands and apply more pressure as defender instinctively rises to his tiptoes to try to relieve pressure.

8. Repeat steps for both right and left sides. Make sure you don't overdue the technique to avoid injury.

REALITY BAR-JUTSU:
COKE NOT SERVED HERE

by James Porco, Creator of Bar-jutsu

With over 16 years as a bar bouncer, I have performed the techniques in this book more times than I can remember. Sure...part of the reason I can't remember them all is because of numerous blows to the head over the years. But what I can remember, I'd like to share with you.

I've learned something new nearly every time I have stepped into a bar. This is especially true each time I've accepted a new bouncer position. We've already discussed the value of preparedness; that is especially important when you find yourself in a new situation.

A bar I had just begun bouncing had a reputation for being a favorite of the local cocaine crowd. One of the reasons I was brought on board was to help clean that problem up. It didn't take long before I had to get to work on that particular to-do item.

During one particularly wicked heat wave, the bar had arranged to bring a local bikini team in as guest bartenders for an evening. It seemed like a great idea. Can you think of anything better on a hot night than cold beer served by bikini team bartenders? Well, one particular patron thought he had a better idea. He began to repeatedly approach one of these girls with offers of cocaine for sexual favors.

One of the obligations of a bouncer is to try to diffuse situations without the use of violence if at all possible (sound familiar?). At the request of the bartender, I approached the patron, explained my opposition

Bar-jutsu says: If an intoxicated opponent's behavior seems too good to be true, it probably is. Remain aware and on guard for as long as the potential for threat remains.

to his marketing idea, and asked him to leave. Surprisingly, he left without incident. Happily and way too politely. His willingness to leave so quietly gave me reason to be suspicious.

Sure enough, within minutes my new friend came storming back into the bar. His demeanor and appearance suggested one of two things:

1) He had just consumed his entire supply of cocaine
2) He had just made a run to Starbuck's and thrown down 3-4 cups of everything they sell.

He ran full-speed into the bar and made a B-line for the spot where we had spoken minutes ago. I was not surprised to see him return. But I needed to be sure that he had nothing in store that *would* surprise me. Again, being aware and prepared is absolutely vital. Rather than avoid him, I accepted that his behavior was now an act of aggression. I decided to match his enthusiasm and take the surprise to him. I ran as well. Directly toward him. The thinking was to subdue his arms before he could pull a knife, gun, or any other weapon.

I placed my left hand on his right wrist, preventing him from punching or grabbing me (Note: when in doubt, play the odds and assume that your opponent is right-handed). From this position I was able to place him into a front-face headlock and push him outside of the bar. Moving the scuffle outside was merely an obligation I had as a bouncer... you should never feel compelled to take an opponent away from the scene of the initial aggression.

Bar-jutsu says: Although it may seem noble, never suggest taking the fight outside. This puts you at risk and gives your attacker a chance to prepare. The situation should always be resolved where it started.

Once outside I was able to "hop" to reposition myself so that my back faced his front. Using the momentum of the hop, I planted my feet and hip-tossed him up and over and down to the concrete. As he lay on the sidewalk, I applied another choke with my right arm while holding his right arm to the ground with my left hand. He fought for a minute as I squeezed my body against the choke. But the hold was effective enough to subdue him until the police responded to someone's 9-1-1 call.

Being aware of my surroundings and being prepared was a key for me here. As it turns out, my attacker was not carrying a weapon. But I was not prepared to make that assumption, and nor should you. By remaining aware I was able to immediately notice his reentry to the bar, and by being prepared I was able to react well before he could.

I hope you never encounter this type of a maniac on your night out. But no matter what you find out there, stay prepared. And have fun!

LESSON 4:

HAVE YOU GOT THE TIME?

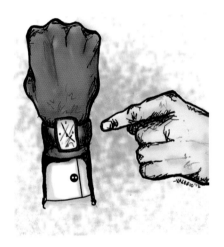

You've been working very diligently on your lessons to this point. Don't think we haven't noticed. We're very impressed, and think you deserve some down time. After all, martial arts and self-defense training is about more than physical training. It's about having a clear and focused mind. So take some "you" time. Meditate. Relax. Let your mind wander a bit. Think happy thoughts. Imagine you are doing something that you really enjoy.

On second thought, hold those thoughts. We know where you might be going with them, and frankly we're a little grossed out. Maybe you'd better let us handle this instead.

How about this: imagine that you are comfortably seated in your favorite bar. Two strategically-located TV's make it possible for you to simultaneously watch both the football and hockey games. You're enjoying a big-boy beverage and some loaded nachos. You use commercial breaks to read up on your Bar-jutsu book (see what happens when you let us take over your happy thoughts?). Except for occasionally signaling the bartender to order another beer, you are keeping to yourself and minding your own business.

Sounds nice, doesn't it? Not so fast. Happy time is over. Here comes reality, and he's had one (OK, five) too many. Turns out reality is actually a distraught drunkard who staggers up to you and accuses you of…

Wait for it…

It's going to sound strange…

Stealing his dog.

Sounds crazy? That's what we thought too when it happened to us a few years ago. After laughing at the realization that a stolen dog would technically be a "hot" dog, we proceeded to handle the situation.

You may like your original meditative happy thought more than ours, but ours is much more realistic than you might think. The truth is that there are all sorts of people out there, and sometimes these people walk into a bar. Sometimes the weird get weirder as they drink. And just when you think you have seen it all, someone accuses you of stealing his dog.

The Bar-light Zone

On some nights it may feel like you stepped into another dimension when you stepped into the bar. In "The Bar-light Zone," time may seem warped. People may seem warped. Some things may seem just too weird to be true. Like meeting someone who insists that you copped his canine.

Weird and bizarre can seem funny at first. But we have seen many situations where bizarre turned bad in the blink of an eye. We've seen someone attack someone with a plastic spork. We've seen a woman remove her top and try to strangle someone with it. We've even watched a good clown go bad (more on that later).

And yes, we've had someone come after us for pinching his pooch.

When you encounter weirdness in The Bar-light Zone, your first reaction may be to laugh it off and move on. Sure, the behavior may keep you occupied for a moment or two. But we know your attention span. You've got more pressing matters to attend to. Soon your mind is back to the important business of your nachos, where you were busy identifying a chip shaped like each state of the union before being rudely interrupted. And in all the commotion, you may have accidentally eaten Iowa.

But you soon accept the fact that tonight you are in The Bar-light Zone, where it is easy to find characters that are laughable. They drink. They act goofy. They say the darndest things. Drunken distraught people are so cute at this age. But they're not dangerous. Right?

Wrong. No matter how laughable someone's behavior is, there is still potential to escalate. In fact, bizarre behavior is even more of a reason to be on alert. If someone is emotionally disturbed enough to randomly accuse you of some nonsense, then there is absolutely no reason to give him the benefit of the doubt and or to discount their capacity to do something much worse.

Odd behavior may seem funny. You may even feel sorry for the person. In the great dog-snatching case, for example, it's obvious that your accuser is either:

Bar-jutsu says: Never underestimate odd behavior or peculiar situations, even if all appears harmless. "Odd" is often a precursor to "angry." Angry often attacks.

a) Very disturbed
b) Very hammered
c) Very distraught over the whereabouts of Rex, to the point that you are questioning the true nature of their relationship.

At times like this it is easy to let your guard down or to under-estimate the potential for danger. Your brain may be saying "There's nothing to see here, move along." And most times you may be right. It may just be a momentary spectacle. But bizarre behav-ior can in fact be very dangerous. Bizarre is bad; bizarre in a bar is even worse. No one can predict the effect alcohol will have on a troubled mind.

Sometimes it is just about timing. It is like walking past a pot of water simmering on the stove top. When you see it, it may just be blowing off a little steam. Or, if your timing is bad, you may be there when the lid blows and it becomes a hot boiling dangerous mess.

Speaking of timing, this seems like a great time to introduce a maneuver we call "*Have You Got the Time?*" It's a cute little name to help you remember the basics of the move, which resemble an arm twist as if looking at someone's wristwatch. OK, maybe it's not so cute. But neither is the dog lover that just approached you. Re-gardless, this maneuver can be helpful in situations when you are confronted by someone whose behavior in unpredictable.

Setting the Scene: Have You Got the Time?

We've set most of this one up for you already. Recall that you were headed down a more risqué line of thinking before we reeled you in to focus on something more relevant. You. A bar. Two televi-sions. Nachos shaped like states. Demented dog lover. Hopefully this sounds familiar. Maybe a little weird, but familiar.

Anyway, back at the bar you have tried to laugh off the bizarre accusation that you have stolen someone's dog. After being ap-proached and accused, you did all the things that would make us proud. You politely denied the accusation. You suggested that your accuser might have you confused with someone else. You expressed sympathy to him for the loss of his best friend. You've been polite and shown restraint.

Still, he continues to make his case against you. At this point you are a little worried that other patrons may overhear and begin to wonder if you really **did** steal the dog. After all, the guy is pretty convincing.

Finally, you stand and attempt to walk away. As you do so, he grabs your shoulder angrily.

Oh-oh.

The stakes have just gotten a little higher. Remember your training from Lesson 2: physical contact should immediately raise a red flag in your mind. You should now be in self-defense mode.

Introduction to the Maneuver

1. Turn to face the aggressor.

2. Bring your left hand up—with the back of your hand up against the inside of his wrist. (Assuming he grabbed you with his right hand.) At the same time, step back and to the left with your left foot. This will tip his balance, break his concentration, and prevent a possible punch from his left hand. Instead of grabbing you, he will be inclined to try to regain his balance. Destroying his balance is important because it will not allow him to reset and defend himself properly.

3. While turning your upper body to your left, punch through and soften his elbow with your fist. Punching through his elbow is an option. The goal of the punch is to "soften" or dislocate his elbow, making his grip weaker.

4. If you choose not to punch, you can swing your arm underneath and up, like a pendulum. The punch, which is optional, should come

from chest level and straight out, targeting the inside of the elbow.

5. After you punch through **or** use the pendulum motion and swing through, bring your hand up and place your forearm against the back of his elbow. Drag your forearm down to roll his arm away from you. As you drag your arm, slightly squat down with the drag. This will help the roll.

6. Once you have rolled his arm, cup the crook of his elbow and raise your body. Make sure that you maintain your own balance and proper footing. Keeping your back straight and never bending forward or backward is important. If you bend, you could lose your balance and lose complete control of the situation. You would be giving him an opportunity to regain his balance and possibly take over in the fight.

7. Now that you have grabbed the elbow, turn your upper body as you rise and square up with him again. Your left wrist will trap his right wrist, actually locking it in place. Do not arm wrestle with

the attacker. Use your entire body to bend his arm. As your body turns, his arm will give. If you try to use only your arms, you will be in a wrestling match all night. The entire body is the key to making this technique effective.

8. Once he is thrown off balance again you will see him bending backwards to try to stop the pain he is feeling in his elbow. You can now join your hands as if you are looking at his watch.

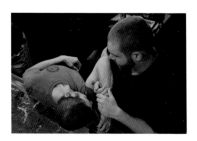

PRACTICING THE MANEUVER

1. Start by squaring up with your partner. Stand at arm's length from each other. The attacker will grab the defender by the shirt collar or shoulder, firmly gripping him, not letting go. It is important that you do not release the grab throughout the technique. You want to train as if you were actually in this confrontation. A loose grip will make the move ineffective. Dedicate yourself to the grab as if you really intend on attacking your opponent.

2. Grab with your right hand.

3. As the defender, step back and to the left at a 45 degree angle. Your back foot should point away from the attacker. Do not step too far. You want a comfortable stance with your knees slightly bent. Because people are built differently, the distance you step will vary. Too much and you will be out of control and lose your balance. Too little and he will retain his balance. Get a feel for what's right for you and what makes him jerk forward, then move on.

4. As you step back and to the left, simultaneously bring your left hand up, placing the back of your hand against the inside of his wrist, gently. Do not grab. When you grab an attacker you give him the impression that you are about to fight back, aggressively. You want to use little energy so that he gets the feeling that you are not the aggressive type.

5. Now turn your upper body counter-clockwise, so that your chest lines up parallel with his arm, but not up against his arm. When you turn, you have the option of delivering the strike to the inside of his elbow or swinging the arm like a pendulum. Let's look at the punch.

6. When you turn, punch straight out from your chest and use the momentum of the turn to drive the force behind the punch. Always punch with your body. A jab from your elbow won't do the trick.

(For training purposes, punch below the elbow, simulating a direct hit.) Once you have punched the elbow, the attacker's arm should loosen slightly, simulating a dislocated elbow, but not releasing the grip. When using the pendulum method, swing the arm with the turn of your body. Try to make all movements at once.

7. Bring your hand up to face level, opening the hand with your thumb pointing toward your face. You want an open hand so that when you roll his arm your hand will fall into the crook of his elbow.

8. As you lower your body, his arm will roll and he will bend backwards. Cup the crook of his elbow and rotate your upper body clockwise, back to its original position. Try to do these moves simultaneously. Start slowly, then at about half speed. As you rotate your body, start to slowly rise to a standing position.

Reposition yourself where you are comfortable, balanced, and out of reach from any type of strikes or retaliation. Once in position, if necessary, step on the back of his knee to lower him to the ground. Otherwise, the pressure applied should cause him to lower.

9. Keep your back straight and remember to breathe throughout the technique. Bending will cause you to lose your balance which could allow your opponent a chance to regain his. Now that you have control, you can lower your body and apply more pressure downward on the lock, taking him to the ground. Moving your body up and down throughout and maintaining your balance will keep him unbalanced and out of the game.

LESSON 5:

UP AGAINST THE WALL

Walls really get a raw deal. On a good day, they get taken for granted. On a bad day, they get things thrown at them. They're on the wrong side of all sorts of argument fodder from our significant others, like "quit putting up walls" or "you drive me right up a wall" (we get that one a lot). And if all this isn't enough, they also have to hold pictures of your dearly departed relatives all day long (including those from the "old country," where the government apparently outlawed smiling).

But walls can be so much more. Take bar walls, for example. On occasion, you've probably found yourself relying on one. If you've had too much to drink, a wall can be a steady friend in need. Many restroom walls are willing to share some rather interesting philosophy. The walls can also be great perches to watch the crowd from.

Of course, watching the crowd can sometimes lead to watching someone else's date. And watching someone's date can lead to someone backing you against a wall. Or trying to mount your head upon the wall, right next to the giant moose head popularly known to customers as "Mr. Moose-n-stein."

An attacker may think they have you at a disadvantage by backing you against a wall. But in the realm of self-defense, a wall can in fact be a handy ally. If you think of yourself as Batman (and we freely admit that we often do this), then think of the wall as Robin. No offense to your friends, but the wall is the only one that can truly have your back. No one else can guarantee the prevention of a sneak attack. If you are positioned against a wall, you have just cut in half the amount of space you need to defend. When positioned properly against a wall, the "field of defense" is now 180 degrees instead of 360 degrees.

Bar-jutsu says: If you position yourself properly against a wall, you can cut in half the amount of space you need to defend in a confrontation, reducing the field of defense from 360 degrees to 180 degrees.

But Robin did more than just defend Batman's flank from surprise attacks by the Joker's goons. Likewise, the wall can handle a little more responsibility than defense of your blind side. If handled properly, you can actually use the wall to help you subdue an attacker.

Of course, the wall is not some stoic personal bodyguard or trusty concealed weapon. Walls have limits. If you are outnumbered, the wall can be a bad place to be. If someone is coming at you with a weapon, a wall can limit your mobility and therefore your ability to defend yourself.

Also, we are in no way suggesting that you should go running for the wall at the first sign of trouble. That would be a little weird. Nor should you point to the wall if someone is giving you a hard time and say something like "My friend here doesn't like the way you're speaking to me." That would be a LOT weird.

What we are suggesting is that if you find yourself between a rock and a hard wall, things are not necessarily as bleak as they might seem. There is a way to use the situation to your advantage.

We're Not Physicists, But We Know What Matters

Gather 'round children, and we will teach you a quick physics lesson. It seems that the science of physics has certain laws, and one of them states that an object at rest will stay at rest unless enough force is applied to it.

So, you push against a beer bottle with enough force, it moves. You apply enough force to a bar stool, it tips over. The more massive the object, the more energy is needed to move it. Not so difficult, right? Maybe this rocket science stuff isn't exactly rocket science after all.

Unless you are in a place that is in really bad shape, the walls will be the most stationary, immovable objects in the bar (except for "old man Charlie," who has been in the same corner booth since 1989). Because of this, walls can offer a means to subdue without taking your opponent to the ground, which is not always an option. Most every other object in the bar does not have enough mass to resist the energy that you would apply in a scuffle. Tables and chairs are no match for the combined energy of you and your opponent; ditto for vending machines, jukeboxes, windows, and nearly anything else. If you attempt to subdue an attacker against something without enough mass to resist, then you, your attacker and the object are all likely to get damaged.

But not the wall. It isn't going anywhere—at least not until old man Charlie does. It's got plenty of mass. And because of its size and shape, it can distribute the pressure of two human bodies pressing against it. So there is little chance that you are going to bring the walls down. Or go through them.

This seems like a good time to introduce a maneuver we call *Up Against the Wall* (the name "Another Brick in the Wall" was already taken, though we are quite certain that we can take the guys from Pink Floyd in a steel cage match for naming rights). It's a maneuver that is designed to make the most of your surroundings while keeping true to the Bar-jutsu theme of "defend and subdue."

To effectively practice this one (and you will practice…right?), all you will need is a willing friend and a wall. Which, if you've been paying attention, actually means that you have two friends present. Because the morale of this lesson is that the wall can actually be a friend in need. While we don't recommend that you invite the wall to your next birthday bash, we do think you owe him one for always being there. So maybe when you are done reading this, maybe you can show him a little appreciation. Start by taking down the old depressing pictures of the relatives. Or at least make enough room to hang a nice replica of Mr. Moose-n-stein.

Setting the Scene: Up Against the Wall

You and your friends are seated at your favorite corner table in your favorite pub. It's a nice little table, close enough to the action to see everything, yet out of the way enough to allow your friend Neckbone to do any number of embarrassing things he is known to do.

But right now, you'd really appreciate it if Neckbone would behave, despite the isolation of your perch. Because nearby is seated the woman you love. The woman you have been faithfully devoted to for over 10 minutes, ever since she and her date showed up.

Undaunted by the competition, you do what any mature gentlemanly would-be suitor would do. You stare at her. And so do your friends. Stares lead to comments, which start to sound dangerously like jeers. Especially once Neckbone gets warmed up.

Soon the woman of your dreams is agitated (she's really going to have to learn to accept your friends). And then you learn something about her that you never knew before; when she gets agitated, so does her hulk boyfriend.

His fury leads him to make a scene, and he angrily approaches you. At first you are amused, mostly because Neckbone has started singing "My Boyfriend's Back." But your opponent finds nothing funny. He's ready to show off a little, and is in no mood to accept an apology.

Her boyfriend's back, and he's gonna be in trouble. He makes a move to push you against the wall. He is unaware that the wall is your friend. And it's a good thing you can count on the wall, because your other friends are no help. Neckbone is writing out your last will and testament on a napkin.

Since your opponent in romance has chosen to place hands on you in anger, he is now your opponent in battle. You should now be ready to defend yourself. And you can do so by introducing him to the wall.

Introduction to the Maneuver: Up Against the Wall

1. The attacker approaches you and starts the confrontation. He grabs you with both hands.

2. You are up against a wall with no room to step back. So you calmly put your hands up, signaling him that you meant no disrespect, meanwhile putting your hands in position to defend yourself.

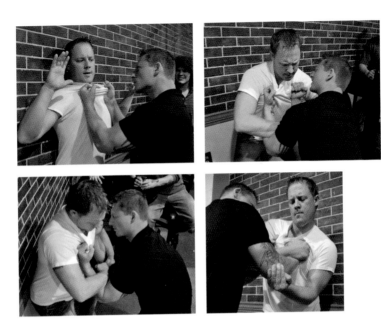

3. As he grabs you, you make two fists and come crashing down on the tops of both of his elbows, bending your knees slightly and lowering your body. This double strike will help weaken his grip.

4. Once you strike, slide your right arm across your chest, trapping his clinched grip against your body. The nice thing about the slide and trap is that he thinks you are trying to pry his hands free, so he will continue to grab you. In his head, he has pinned you against the wall and has complete control of the situation. In reality, he is setting himself up for submission.

5. Bring your left hand down and cup his right elbow. Cupping, not grabbing, will assist in the rotation, allowing the elbow to move freely in your palm.

6. Rotate his arm clockwise and step to your left. Now you can drive him straight into the wall you were just up against. Remember to keep your back straight and don't forget to breathe.

7. To lock out the move, keep applying pressure to the elbow, pushing it inward. Pushing too much will hyper extend it, and pushing too little will allow him to slip off and away from you. Make sure you keep control of him as you politely talk him into calming down.

PRACTICING THE MANEUVER:

1. Both partners stand at arm's length across from each other squared at the shoulders. Defender should stand with back to a wall/fence/tree/etc.

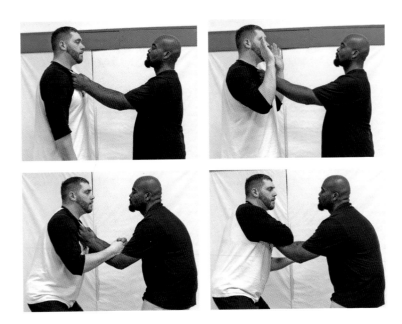

2. Attacker grabs with both hands and pushes against wall.

3. Defender slightly raises hands to show no signs of fighting back.

4. Defender brings hands crashing down on crooks of the elbows while simultaneously lowering the entire body at the knees. (The attacker must maintain a firm grip throughout the technique simulating an actual fight.)

5. Defender slides right hand across chest, trapping attacker's grabbing hands against his body and grabbing the right hand; at the same time sliding the left hand to the attacker's right elbow, cupping it.

6. Defender now slides right leg back and turning clockwise, stepping out away from the wall and raising the body. At the same time, maintain grip of attacker's trapped right hand and rotating his elbow upwards.

7. Turn your upper body so that it is parallel to the attacker's right arm and apply pressure to the back of the right elbow, forcing him against the wall.

Repeat steps for both right and left sides. Also try this move while not standing against an object.

LESSON 6:

IS THAT A BROKEN BEER BOTTLE IN YOUR HAND, OR ARE YOU JUST HAPPY TO SEE ME?

So what is it about guys and bottles anyway? As infants, one of the first things we learn to reach for is a bottle. When we go to our first junior-high party, the first thing we suggest playing is spin-the-bottle. Once we're old enough to have a bad day at work, we can't wait to get home so that we can reach for a bottle. And when we walk into a bar, what's the first thing we reach for? A blonde. But one slap across the face later, the next thing we reach for is a bottle.

Unfortunately, bars and bottles aren't always as warm and fuzzy as babies and bottles. For most of the evening a bottle is actually our friend; it holds our favorite beverage for us; it lets us lift it high in the air to help show approval of the band; and it rarely leaves our side. But every once in awhile fun turns to fight, and someone tries to turn our friend against us.

You may recall from the Introduction of this book that we hold Hollywood partially responsible for misconceptions about bar fights. Hollywood does to bar fights what Photoshop does to pictures. It can hide a good deal of ugly. Watch an old Western movie and you're likely to see someone in a saloon laughingly break a bottle of the good stuff over someone's head for "a-cheatin" at cards. Or maybe someone cracks a bottle over the edge of a table and starts brandishing the makeshift weapon like they are suddenly King Arthur wielding Excalibur.

However, even John Wayne and King Arthur would agree that a broken bottle is nothing to laugh at. The sharp edge of a broken glass bottle may not be a knife blade, but it can slash and cause the same types of serious injuries. The average bar patron may not walk in carrying a weapon. But anyone can create one in a matter of seconds, and the broken bottle is very often the do-it-yourself weapon of choice.

In *Lesson 4: Have You Got the Time*, we stressed the importance of taking serious anyone whose behavior is bizarre, even if the events playing out seem humorous at first. This point is just as valid here. So if the site of an incoherent, stumbling guy coming at you with a sawed-off wine cooler seems funny to you, stay focused. You can laugh later.

Of course the weapon will not always be a bottle. You may not even view it as a weapon, and therefore you may not immediately see any danger. You don't need to. It's the angry attacker that is the real weapon, and they will find a way to use just about anything to their advantage, even if it is merely to distract you. In the split second it takes for someone to come at you, you simply don't have time to determine if the weapon is a real threat or not. In fact, we'll make the decision for you: if an opponent is threatening you in any way with any sort of object at all, that object is a danger to you. From the moment an attacker grabs anything with the intent to use it in a violent manner, you should consider yourself to be engaged in a highly dangerous situation.

Bar-jutsu says: The very minute that an aggressor grabs any object with the intent to use it in violence, you should consider yourself in a highly dangerous situation.

A very important distinction needs to be made here. While we are suggesting that any type of object being used as a weapon should be taken seriously, there is one category of weapons that warrants extra consideration. Obviously there is a big difference between a bottle and a handgun. A primary concern when dealing with any confronter should be the potential that he may be carrying a concealed **deadly** weapon.

Guns and knives are extra-serious threats. You should **never** attempt to disarm someone who is brandishing one of these weapons unless they have made it very clear that your life—or that of another—is clearly in danger otherwise. Nor should you match weapon for weapon, drawing yours if you happen to be carrying one. This is not the old West. Anything that instigates an armed opponent may prompt him to use his weapon. This is exactly what you should be trying to avoid at all costs.

Bar-jutsu says: Deadly weapons are deadly. Never attempt to disarm someone who is brandishing a knife or a gun unless it is very clear that your life is in direct danger if you do not act immediately.

Unless you are very certain that the only way to prevent the attacker from using the deadly weapon is to make a move for it, then the best strategy it to stand down. *Disarmament of deadly weapons is a job for the authorities.* Regardless of which side of the "guns don't kill people, people kill people" fence you stand on, the sad truth is that either way people can wind up getting killed if a deadly weapon shows up. We don't want you to be one of them. We like you. You're part of the Bar-jutsu family. We have big plans for you.

Beware the Barsenal

Recall from *Lesson 1: Making an Entrance* that you should be on alert from the moment you walk into a bar for things that can be used as a weapon. An angry attacker will not be going for style points; he will use anything at his disposal to gain an advantage over you.

A bar has a wide variety of objects that can be used as makeshift weapons in a scuffle. We like to think of this as the "barsenal"—the arsenal full of objects found in bars that are weapons in waiting. A typical barsenal can include pool cue sticks, darts, chairs and stools, metal napkin dispensers, utensils, and plates. All these and more lie in the shadows like silent ninja death stars, waiting for the desperate attacker to reach for them in anger. We've seen people grab for anything in the heat of battle—from signs hanging on the wall to handbags to saltshakers and glass ketchup bottles.

But much in the way that gunslingers reach for their trusty six-shooter when it all hits the fan, it seems like the first choice for many attackers is the beer bottle. It is by far the most common weapon in the barsenal. So let's focus on this weapon of glass destruction.

In the following scenario, you will be faced by an attacker who has decided to draw on you with the broken bottle. While you hate to see someone using your old friend against you like this, you can at least be assured of two things. First, the attacker has no intention of playing spin the bottle with you. And second, this is no movie scene. You are in a very real and very dangerous predicament.

Setting the Scene: Is That a Broken Bottle in Your Hand, or Are You Just Happy to See Me?

You and a friend are hard at work volunteering in a local home for seniors. You do this often, and tonight the two of you are singing folk songs, reciting poetry, and generally entertaining the residents.

OK, relax. You're not really doing any of that. We just wanted to make sure you were paying attention. You two are in a bar. Feel better?

Your friend is seated at the bar, while you are catching up with some old friends at a nearby table. Suddenly you hear a commotion over at the bar. Apparently your friend was singing folk songs, or reciting poetry, or doing something that agitated the guy seated next to him. They are engaged in a heated argument.

As you approach the bar, you see what the commotion is all about. The angry poetry/folk song-hater has broken a bottle and is now aiming it at your friend. As you get closer to the situation, the attacker decides that you are more deserving of his attention.

If you weren't paying attention at the beginning of this scenario, you should be now. You are now facing an armed opponent. He doesn't care if you spend your free time volunteering or not. He only cares where you are right now. Which is the wrong place, at the wrong time.

Fortunately you have learned a few things about the seriousness of an opponent with a dangerous weapon. And how to respond should he attack. So you end up volunteering this evening after all. You volunteer to share a lesson in self-defense with him.

Introduction to the Maneuver: Is That a Broken Bottle in Your Hand, or Are You Just Happy to See Me?

1. Pay attention to the attacker. Is he moving quickly or slowly? Do you anticipate an overhead swing, side swing, or stabbing motion? Study his moves as much as you can.

2. As he holds the bottle in his right hand, he cocks back to swing at you. Like always, be aware of your surroundings.

3. Step in before he finishes the swing and place yourself between your attacker and the weapon.

4. As you step inside, capture his wrist with your left hand and stop the swing.

5. With your right hand "Pie Face" him to blind him and create confusion. Remember to keep your hands open, avoiding grabbing. He will be most likely moving rapidly so if you try to grab, you will commit to that grab and lose focus on the big picture. Only grab at the appropriate time to subdue.

6. When you take his vision away, you will be close enough to use the other parts of your body to finish the technique. You should be close enough to place your right leg behind his right leg and sweep him off his feet.

7. Once he is down, take the broken bottle away. At this point, sit on him and wait until police arrive.

PRACTICING THE MANEUVER:

1. Both partners stand just outside of arm's length away from each other, squared up at the shoulders.

2. Attacker may use unbroken beer bottle or any other non-lethal, safe object to simulate a broken bottle. Slowly raise your arm holding the object and slowly swing from above your head at a 45 degree angle downward.

3. Defender slides in with the right foot before the swing completes or makes its "cut."

4. Keeping your hands open, place your left hand on the attacking wrist and your right hand fanned open on the attacker's face, taking away his vision and distracting him.

5. Once you are in position, grab the wrist, stay close hip to hip, with your right leg just behind his right leg.

6. Since he is basically swinging in a counter-clockwise motion, go with his movement keeping his momentum continuous thus throwing him off balance while you continue to turn. Pushing on his face will also throw him off his game and make it easier to take him to the ground.

Once he is down, place the back of his elbow against your knee and take the weapon away.

7. Repeat steps for both right and left sides.

DID YOU JUST SLAP ME WITH A PICKLE?

*by **Matt Porter**, Professional Bar Bouncer*

I have been a bar bouncer in the city of Pittsburgh, Pennsylvania for over eight years. Most of the people I meet coming into the bar are really great people. They come in to celebrate big events like birthdays or promotions. Sometimes they're with a date, and sometimes they're with a group of friends. I've met some really great people on the job.

But that doesn't change the fact that bouncing is a tough job. On an average night, you may find yourself breaking up a fight, escorting someone out for bothering other patrons, and keeping someone inside until you can get them a cab ride home.

My favorite time of the evening is the "home stretch." The home stretch is the final hour or so when a majority of people have gone home for the night. With only a few "hardcore" folks still hanging in there until last call, the numbers are more in your favor. You can breathe a little easier.

At least that's what I used to think. Then something happened, something that forever changed my view on the home stretch. It happened years ago, but the local townsfolk still speak of it, recanting sketchy details in folk story. But I was there. I saw the whole thing. I survived "Pickle Pandemonium in Pittsburgh."

It all began innocently enough. It was late and the place had emptied considerably. There were about eight guys still standing. Well, not really standing. They'd seen better days by this point, but they had formed a bit of support group to help each other hang in there. They were talking to each other, sharing philosophy on life and having harmless laughs.

As the home of Heinz Foods and countless great sandwiches, Pittsburgh is a town that takes its pickles seriously. It's not uncommon for any bar or restaurant that serves food to get special requests to roll out the pickle barrel. On this particular night, one of the remaining bar guests had convinced the bartender to bring out a big jar of the green goodies so that the gang could enjoy a late-night snack.

For reasons no one understands to this day, one of the group reached deep into the jar for a pickle, withdrew one he believed to be most suitable for a special assignment, and then slapped it across the face of the guy next to him.

Let me repeat...he slapped someone across the face with a pickle.

I'm not sure that there is a rulebook for how to respond to being slapped in the face with a pickle. But I can only think of two things you should *expect* to happen. And on this night, both happened. First, the victim asked the obvious: "*Dude, did you just slap me with a pickle?!?*" Next, a fight broke out.

Again, there were only eight guests in the bar. And yet, all eight felt compelled to answer the call to arms. I suddenly had eight men fighting over one pickle slap across the face. It became the slap heard 'round the bar.

With the odds I was facing, I had to make a judgment call. I could not break up four fights by myself. I decided to make my move for the original aggressor, hopeful that by subduing him the others would feel that some order was being restored.

Sometimes when you intervene in a fight, you run the risk of becoming part of the problem. If you subdue one fighter, his opponent may see that as an opportunity. You become a tag-team partner, and the fighter whose hands are free uses the opportunity to land a blow or two.

With that in mind, my primary object was to take the instigator to the ground, where I could cover him with my own body and effectively take both he and his opponent out of the game. Unless you are a bouncer, I don't advise you to jump in to break up a fight unless you really need to. But if you do, a good idea is to take one of the opponents to the ground and cover him. It is very unlikely the other will try to stop you. Should you ever find yourself in a situation like this, I advise you to do the same...

Eventually the police arrived and order was restored. All eight food fighters found themselves in a real pickle, as charges were pressed and there were damages to the bar to be held account-able for.

I hope you never find yourself in this type of situation. But I guess the lesson to be learned is that you don't need a large crowd for things to get crazy. All you need is a few last-call lingerers. And maybe a jar of pickles.

LESSON 7:
KARAOKE-JUTSU

The wheel. Electricity. The personal computer. Barbeque sauce. All great advancements of science. It is hard to imagine life before these marvels of ingenuity arrived on the scene.

We are also big fans of karaoke, and boldly put it up there with some of mankind's great inventions. Sure, the automobile has had its moments...but what has it ever done to make you feel like a rock star? The light bulb? Important, but has it ever lifted a finger to help give you five minutes of fame?

As promoters of public fun, it should not surprise you that we are in karaoke's corner. It is a stroke of pure genius. Karaoke enables people to do something constructive with all of the courage they accumulated during happy hour. For those willing to grab the mic, karaoke is a chance to realize a dream they've had all of their lives. Or at least it's been a big dream for the past 30 minutes or so, ever since deciding to try the newest drink on the menu, something called the "The Zombie Maker."

Of course, having fun with something doesn't mean that you are good at it. In truth, most of us are lousy singers, even when we're sober. But that's half the fun. This isn't some television show where your golden voice gives you a shot at reality TV fame and fortune. It's just a chance to ham it up with your friends. To walk a mile in Axle Rose's shoes. Or Toby Keith's boots. To dedicate "*I Will Survive*" to your ex, or "*Do Ya Think I'm Sexy?*" to your future ex. It is all about having fun.

Try explaining that to some people. For every bad karaoke singer, there is one waiting impatiently to take his or her place. And another one who has no intention of getting up there, but every intention of making your climb to fame as miserable as possible. We're referring of course to the heckler.

Heckling has ties that go all the way to Japan, the birthplace of karaoke. In fact, the word "heckle" comes from the ancient Japanese phrase "heckle-soto ha-ha-ha-ha-ha fa so la ti do oh oh," meaning "Wow dude, you suck."

There are actually two species of hecklers. The first is the more docile "*armchair heckler.*" Armchair hecklers have much to say, but do not leave the comfort of their seats to say it. They shout things like "somebody please stab that person in the head with a tuning fork and put us all out of our misery." Since these hecklers are actually the friends you came in with, we'll leave dealing with them up to you.

More troublesome is the aggressive "*killer heckler.*" This species is much more active, and will attack if they feel threatened. And should they decide that it is their turn to take the stage—or that they have simply had enough of your rendition of "*Copacabana*"—then they interpret this as a threat. And so should you.

Dr. Heckle and Mr. Hide

It some ways, being attacked on stage is similar to the situation you found yourself in during *Lesson 5: Up Against the Wall*. Typically all of the action is in front of you. There is no real threat of a sneak attack from behind (unless the karaoke DJ snaps and decides to ambush you). So, just as when you find yourself against a wall, your field of defense is likely 180 degrees here as well. You probably are in a bit of a cramped corner as well, with tables or sound equipment around you, limiting mobility.

But there is one particularly important difference. You are in front of a room full of people. A bar full of witnesses. Witnesses bring advantages and disadvantages. On the plus side, the attack is likely to be a brief one. Bouncers, security, or even other patrons won't stand by and watch you being attacked without doing anything—regardless of how badly you sound up there.

However, if Dr. Heckle makes an aggressive move on you, you cannot exactly become Mr. Hide up there. There is little room to retreat. He has you cornered with nowhere to run.

In fact, you may have no interest in a retreat. You are in the spotlight. The spotlight does funny things. We become conscious of what people think of us. Bravado takes over. No one wants to wilt in the spotlight. You may be tempted to make the first aggressive move. With eyes watching, it becomes a matter of "If my singing didn't impress everyone, maybe my right hook will." It is easy to feel suddenly compelled to react. Especially if you were just singing "*Taking Care of Business*" or "*Bad to the Bone*." You have to practice what you were just preaching, right?

Wrong.

Not to sound like a broken record (get it?

Bar-jutsu says: The appropriate approach to self-defense does not vary with the number of eyes on you. Do not respond physically until you are physically attacked, even if there is a crowd watching for your reaction.

Karaoke…record?), but you are only a defender if you are defending. That is what defenders do. Your would-be attacker can insult, heckle, even walk toward you just as you are getting to the best part of your song. None of these things are an attack. And while you may feel embarrassed in front of others, the appropriate response is to avoid the taunts. Do not respond physically, even if it is to put your hand on his shoulder to gently push him out of your light. Want to really get under his skin? Keep singing that song.

However, should he make an aggressive move on you—should he make first contact and actually put a hand on you in a forceful manner—then that is a whole new tune. Now it is appropriate to defend yourself. The song is about to become a dance.

The following maneuver is a great one to consider in a situation like this. It can be performed quickly and will help you subdue just long enough for an authority to take over. And it can be managed even if one hand is occupied with something else (like a micro-phone). And while others may be secretly hoping that you drop the mic by this point, you are a true performer. You know the first rule of show business. The show must go on.

Setting the Scene: Karaoke-jutsu

As with every scenario presented in this book, the following is based on some reality, and some fiction. We re-enact real events that we have witnessed and even participated in. But we change a few facts to hypothetically drop you into the action, and slow things down to demonstrate a few maneuvers.

With that reminder, we now drop you into Karaoke Night at your local bar. It's a fictional scenario. But our lawyers have advised us to avoid straying too far from the truth in these matters. So in the interest of keeping it real, we must warn you that while you are up on stage and singing your heart out, you sound bad. Very bad. Wounded animal bad. Sorry.

Nevertheless, we applaud you (it helps drown the noise out). You're having fun. But someone else doesn't see it that way. You have been on his last nerve all evening. This is, after all, your fifth visit to the stage. We suspect he has started a drinking game re-quiring a shot for each time you miss a key. He is now hammered.

He is on the list to take a turn, but he is growing tired of wait-ing and even more tired of your act. During your previous number, he began armchair heckling you. But now he has become a killer heckler. He approaches the stage.

With four songs under your belt, you are seasoned pro. You have no intention of relinquishing the spotlight before you have finished. Your fans deserve better. However, the killer heckler has made a move—he has grabbed you in a violent manner. You must now find a way to defend yourself without letting your fan base down.

Introduction to the Maneuver: Karaoke-jutsu

1. The attacker grabs your wrist. As he does, you step back, de-stroying his balance. Since you are holding the mike in your life hand in this scenario, you step back and to the left.

2. With your right foot, cross over step to your left and bring your right arm over his right arm, dropping your tricep down onto the crook of his elbow. Allow it to slide into the pocket of your armpit.

3. Step to the left, and lower your body. This will cause his arm to bend slightly. Now that you are in position, reach for his naval with your right hand.

4. Step behind him and grab his collar with your left hand. (By this time he would have released the grip on your wrist.)

5. You can now keep him subdued until order can be restored. In the meantime, you can just keep singing.

PRACTICING THE MANEUVER

1. Both partners stand at arm's length away from each other squared at the shoulders.

2. Attacker can grab with his right hand either the left wrist or arm sleeve.

3. Defender steps back and to the left 45 degrees, destroying the attacker's balance.

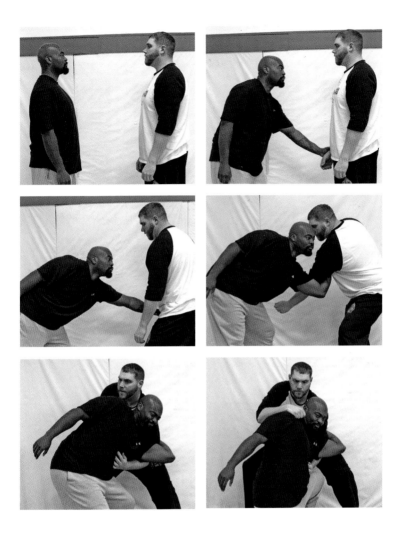

4. Defender performs a right cross over step to the left while bringing his right arm over and down onto the top of the attacker's elbow.

5. As the defender's arm comes down, bend the knees slightly, causing the attacker's arm to bend.

6. Reach down, rotating the arm counter-clockwise and grabbing the attacker's stomach.

7. At this point the attacker will automatically release his grip, freeing your left hand and allowing you to grab his collar as you step behind him and take control.

8. This is a tricky move so take it slow, allow your training partner to bend with you, and make sure to have a safe word or tap to stop if too much strain is involved.

9. Repeat steps for both right and left sides.

I'M NOT AS THINK AS YOU DRUNK I AM

At Bar-jutsu, we're not all about physical maneuvers and defense tactics. We can be cerebral too, and have been known to dabble a little in philosophy. We even have a favorite philosophical quote about life in general: *"Sometimes you're the windshield, sometimes you're the bug."* – Mark Knopfler

As philosophical thinkers ourselves, we have written our own life quote. It goes something like this: *"Sometimes you're the bug, sometimes you're the drunken maniac who relieves yourself on the windshield of someone's Audi."* – Bar-jutsu

For much of this book, we have painted you in a good light. As we've mentioned before, we look out for you; you are part of the Bar-jutsu family now. We like you. So we've focused on your role as a self-defender and a peacekeeper. The scenarios have made the assumption that you are the victim of an aggression. The good guy, who was just minding your own business when you were attacked.

But in reality, life can be a little more complicated than that. And by "complicated," we mean that sometimes you can be a real jerk.

Don't feel too badly. It happens to all of us. It would be completely naïve of us—and of you—to think that you will never cross the line. Your intentions are good enough. You plan on walking into the bar for a few drinks with your friends. Just some laughs. It's been a rough week. Two beers into the evening, you admit to your friends that you've never tried tequila. They'll have none of that, so before you know it the bartender is pouring a shot of tequila just for you. And it's not bad, so you have eight more. Before you know it you are tearfully remembering Sasha, who left you 27 months and 3 days ago this very night. So you try to get the entire place to join you in a rendition of "*Let's Stay Together.*" This brings a nasty look and a few not-so-under-the-breath comments from someone who is annoyed by your behavior (and your voice). Soon words are exchanged. After all, nobody disrespects Al Green on your watch.

So, you may or may not have said something to him. And that something may or may not have been along the lines of "Shut up… don't interrupt an Al Green song…you're just jealous because I had Sasha and all you have is Sasquatch there with you. Or is that your mom?"

Just that quickly, bad blood is born. And as much as we love you, we have to say it: you started it. Tomorrow you will realize that. You will also realize that too much tequila can leave you feeling as though you had a blood transfusion, but they were all out of blood and settled for pancake syrup.

Honey, Take Out The Trash Talk

We've spent a good deal of time reminding you to avoid being an aggressor. Remember, attackers attack, and defenders defend. But it is also important to note that you do not have to violate the Bar-jutsu basic of first contact to be an aggressor. You can instigate aggression just as easily by non-physical behavior.

If imitation is the sincerest form of flattery, then instigation is the sincerest way to ask someone to hit you. Instigation simply mimics the behavior of an attacker. In all

Bar-jutsu says: Provoking aggression is no better than starting it. Never instigate aggression. First contact is only one way to instigate. Taunts, stare-downs, insults, and rudeness all can provoke an attack.

instances, your goal should be to avoid the scuffle. The fact that someone else takes the first swing makes them wrong for sure. But the fact that you fired the first shot lays a good deal of blame at your doorstep as well.

The Bar-jutsu research division has uncovered an interesting fact regarding this. It seems that a vast majority of women hate trash talkers. Women prefer a man who is cool, confident, and can show restraint. One who will defend when necessary, but otherwise will remain quietly in control. The infamous strong, silent type. Of course they also wouldn't mind if he looked like Brad Pitt, had a foreign accent like Fabio, cooked like Emeril, and gave great foot massages. But we can only do so much. We'll help you with the restrained self-defense part now. The rest will have to wait for a different book, like maybe *Bar-jutsu: The Miracle Worker*.

Of course our wives and girlfriends aren't the only ones who wish we'd curb the trash talk and rude behavior. Would-be attackers aren't so crazy about it either. And since they are not students of Bar-jutsu, we cannot expect them to show the same restraint that you have learned to wield. So if you provoke them enough, you can expect them to snap. They will do what attackers do. And you will have to be prepared to defend. Even though you instigated the reaction.

Let's take a look at another maneuver. This one is especially helpful for two reasons. One, it is easy enough to manage in a weakened state, such as the one you might find yourself in 30 minutes after drinking too much tequila. Two, it is a good defense technique to use against an opponent who is fueled by blind rage and who assumes you are too far gone to put up any sort of defense.

In other words, while you have spent most of your Bar-jutsu training to this point being the windshield, someone is about to try to make you the bug. But you can still fly away unscathed. We'd prefer both you and your attacker follow the advice of Al Green, who preached for love whether "times are good or bad, happy or sad." But sometimes the bad times call for a little tough love. And you are about to get a dose.

Setting the Scene: I'm Not as Think as You Drunk I Am

Question: How many shots of tequila are too many?
　　Answer: Yes
　　It seemed like a good idea at the time, but eight tequila shots later, you are making no sense. You are your usual lovable self, just not thinking very clearly. You've done no real harm, just grown a little weird as the night has proceeded. Loud singing, tearful trips down memory lane, and insults to those who dared ask that you and your tequila tone it down.
　　Mercifully, your friends have decided to stop the fight. They throw in the towel and prepare your escape. While one friend brings the car around back, another helps you out. Fortunately you are also friends with the management, who have allowed you to use the rear exit to avoid any further incidents with the rest of the crowd. Especially the one guy that you already came close to blows with.
　　Your friend walks you to the rear of the bar, where you convince her that you are able to make the rest of the walk of shame yourself. You begin a perilous walk down a ramp and to your ride, who is waiting to drive you home to your hangover.
　　On your way out, you run into him. The guy who least enjoyed your first-ever encounter with tequila. Already irritated by you, he

is happy to see you hurting a little. But he tries one last time to be a sport, asking if you are OK. By now you are not OK, and say something that isn't very nice. We figured you wouldn't remember afterward exactly what you said, so we wrote it down for you. It was, and we quote,

"I'm not as think as you drunk I am, but your Chewbacca-girl is as think as I ugly she is."

His bogus concern turns to real anger. Thinking you are an easy target, he prepares to give you a head start on your pending headache.

He underestimates your training, which by now is instinctive to you (since you have practiced so frequently...right?). Despite your condition, you are prepared to defend yourself from an attacker. Though you probably deserve a little tough love right now, an attack is more tough than love. So you again find yourself in self-defense mode.

Introduction to the Maneuver:
I'm Not as Think as You Drunk I Am

1. Your attacker takes a swing at you. He believes he has an advantage over you in your weakened state.

2. As he takes his swing you move slightly to the outside of the punch, just missing it. The less energy you use the better.

3. As the punch passes, follow it with your opposite hand. So, if he throws a right, follow with a left. Using a circular motion, guide his hand downward and then back. Slide into him so that your side is against his side. His arm will end up trapped between your shoulder and your head.

4. Drive your elbow into his shoulder blades. As you force downward, lower your right knee and extend your left knee straight out and behind you, sweeping his right leg.

5. Once he drops feel free to sit on him (if there is a need to subdue), keeping his arm locked in place.

6. Now you can either wait for someone to arrive and assist you, talk him out of resisting any further, or simply take his shirt and be on your way.

PRACTICING THE MANEUVER:

1. Both partners standing just outside of arm's length away.

2. Attacker throws a right punch aiming for the defender's face. Defender steps just to the outside of the punch, bringing your left hand up and placing the back of your left hand onto the back of the attacker's right hand.

3. Rotate your arm down in a clock-wise motion in front of your body, driving the punch down and behind the attacker.

4. Once the punch is blocked and out of the way, slide in with your left foot so that it ends up behind him, bringing you hip to hip and locking his right arm between your head and left shoulder.

5. Place your left elbow onto his shoulder blades, keeping your back straight and take your left arm and swing it down at 45 degrees. If needed, sweep out his right leg with your left leg. Be extremely careful and allow defender to roll or fall without injury. Slow and controlled.

6. Repeat steps for both right and left sides.

RADIO ALMOST KILLED A VIDEO STAR

by **John Karl**, Private Security/Bodyguard

I have worked in private security for most of my professional career. In that capacity I have had a variety of security duties, including assignment as a personal bodyguard. I have worked with business executives, politicians, visiting foreign dignitaries, and celebrities. For the most part the job has been a relatively low-key one. I know not everyone in this line of work can say the same, but I have been fortunate enough to work with clients who do not typically find themselves in much trouble. In fact, my role has primarily been one of keeping other troublemakers away. My clients have been the types that look for privacy when they are out and enjoy the peace of mind that comes with having personal security present.

And then, there is "Celebrity Client X."

I was once assigned to a celebrity client who seemed to have a gift for finding trouble. I will not use his name here, but here's a hint: he is an actor, and has a penchant for partying hard and getting in trouble. OK, I know that may not narrow the field much. Sorry, but part of success in this line of work is discretion.

On one particular New Year's Eve, I was asked to accompany this client to a private party. There was to be a large crowd there, and the hosts had arranged for security. Nevertheless my client wanted me there as a precaution. Professionally, I hate parties. Large crowds, noise, and other variables all make it tough to do the job. Worse yet, it was New Year's Eve and I was with a client who was likely to be intoxicated before even arriving at the door.

Officially my job was to stick nearby and keep an eye on the crowd. Unofficially I knew that my real job was to keep an eye on my client. I knew I was in trouble early on; as we arrived he kept asking everyone "So whose birthday is it again?"

But a few hours into the party, I was feeling better. Other than spilling a drink, my client seemed to be in control of himself and there were no real incidents. I stuck close enough to keep an eye on him, but far enough away to not crowd his space. Every once in a while I would parole the room and the grounds of the club to keep an eye on the big picture.

I took one of these walks and made my way toward the back of the club. The mood was jovial but not really boisterous. It wasn't a particularly noisy crowd, and the lines of site were good. That would prove to help. From the back of the room I noticed a commotion toward the front. Somehow, I just knew that I would find my client in the thick of this. I ran full speed toward where I last left him, pushing people out of the way. As I got closer I could hear him screaming obscenities. I was prepared to pull him off of someone when got there.

When I made it to the scene, I saw that someone had my client in an armlock. The screams were screams of pain; his attacker was applying downward pressure on the arm, driving him to the floor.

I immediately reached around from behind, wrapping my arm under the attacker's arm to alleviate the pressure he was placing on my client. In turn, my opponent hooked my left leg with his own and drove backward, attempting to disrupt my balance.

Oh-oh. This guy knew what he was doing!

As I struggled with the attacker, I noticed a radio on his chest. Within seconds, another radio-wearing attacker approached me from behind and applied his own armlock, trying desperately to pull me away.

At that moment…with four guys all locked together in a human tug of war, I realized what was going on. I was actually engaged with party security. I had no intention of releasing my grip; my first duty was still to protect my client. But I calmly explained that I was private security for the guy at the front of this human chain, and we all mutually agreed to release.

As it turns out, my fun-loving client had noticed a radio on the original "attacker," and decided that he was going to use it to wish everyone a Happy New Year. He grabbed for the transmitter, prompting the armlock that created the chain reaction that became party security history.

I doubt my client remembers this story. He probably didn't even remember it the next morning. But I hope that somehow he learned a lesson, and I hope you can benefit from it as well. Reaching without warning for anything that is on another person is an invitation for trouble. It can easily be interpreted as an attack, even if the motive is as innocent as spreading holiday cheer.

So keep your hands to yourself…unless you are defending yourself from someone. Like perhaps a celebrity well-wisher.

LESSON 9:

WHO IS THIS CLOWN?

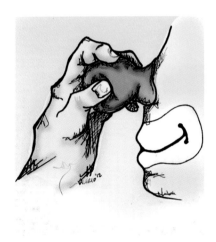

Lesson 9! You have made tremendous progress. We're very proud of you. In fact, we'd like to reward you for the dedication and commitment you have shown to this point. So we have a little "something-something" for you.

If you turn the page, one of our favorite *Bar-jutsu Girls* is waiting with a personal message just for you. She is equally impressed by your progress, and has come up with a very special way of showing you. You don't want to keep her waiting, so turn the page. We'll wait here until you're back.

...

  ...

    ...

Yeah, that was not very nice of us. Professional wrestler Mike Blade probably isn't real happy with us calling him a Bar-jutsu Girl, either. Sorry. We can be real jerks sometimes.

But if you'll work with us here, you'll see that we're simply trying to prove a point. Sometimes jokes just aren't funny. They may seem hilarious to you, but someone else just isn't feeling it. In fact, they may feel like the punch line.

Don't judge us by the bad one-liners we've written in this book. We are actually huge fans of funny. Including pranks and practical jokes. Isn't that one of the reasons you headed out for the night anyway? To get together with friends and laugh? Humor is one of the cornerstones of Bar-jutsu.

Bars are tailor-made for laughter. For some people, a few drinks is all they need to find anything funny. We've seen people laugh hysterically at everything from the menu to floating ice cubes. And we think that is just great.

But sometimes laughs cross a line. The jokes become offensive. Or a prank goes one step too far. Suddenly a joke isn't just a joke anymore. The class clown becomes an ass-clown. And a joke becomes something else. In effect, the joke becomes a perceived attack act of instigation. And you already know how we feel about instigators.

We have also repeatedly advised you to consider humor in a confrontational situation. It can help lighten the mood and relieve tensions. But be careful not to take it too far. Your opponent may feel like you are egging him on. There is a big difference between "funny" and "smartass."

Bar-jutsu says: Humor can be an ally that helps to diffuse a tense confrontation. It can also be a foe, helping to instigate confrontation. Be mindful of your use of humor. Laugh with your opponent, never at him.

Booze-o the Clown

As with so many other situations we have examined, there really is no way of predicting what kind of zaniness alcohol will bring to a table. This is particularly true when the jokes are flying. You may remember "pull my finger" as the funniest prank ever, even though as a child your father used to humiliate you by asking your friends to take turns doing it. But try it now on the wrong someone who has been drinking the wrong something, and the reaction may be a tearful *"My grandmother died that way, you heartless bastard!"*

Alcohol affects everyone differently. But more often than not, it heightens emotions. It can make happy happier, or sad sadder. And if you laugh too hard at someone else's expense, it can make for angry company.

We don't want to sound like your mom or Ms. Manners, but sometimes an apology is all that is needed. A simple "I'm sorry" to show you are not the jerk that your joke says you are. The Bar-jutsu Research Division has determined that nine times out of ten, a sincere apology can smooth over hard feelings.

The tenth time? That's the one you need to be prepared for. If you have created enough hard feelings, the tenth time could become the time that someone thinks the joke should be on you. Hurt feelings, anger, or just embarrassment can be enough to bring the situation to blows. And then it's more punch than punch line.

Bars are perfect places for laughs. But a bad reaction to jokes, pranks, and other people's laughter is not so welcome there. You just don't expect to find many tears in a bar. Nor should you expect to find much anger there. But the very last thing you would probably ever expect to find there? A drunken, angry, violent circus clown.

We swear, we are not making this up. Like every other lesson in this book, the inspiration came from a real life scenario. This one seems so bizarre that we feel the need to reiterate that. This is reality. We're not clever enough to make this up.

The story goes something like this…once upon a time a group of guys gathered in a bar for a bachelor party. They thought of everything. Friends? Check. Private room behind the bar? Check. Food and drink? Check.

Entertainment? Well, that's where the story gets complicated.

The customary exotic dancer was there. But this outgoing bachelor was so loved by his friends that they felt that one dancer wasn't enough. They promised him a second. One that would give him special attention. The group sat the man of the hour in a special seat, and called the lovely little lady out.

Turns out that dancer #2 was in fact a professional circus clown. In full costume.

This may only garner a chuckle out of you while reading about it. But the scene of a clown walking into a bachelor party was an invitation to chaos for this group. The look on the face of the eager groom alone was enough to bring the entire drunken room to their knees. They laughed hysterically. They taunted. Even the bar staff whooped it up. You could hear the commotion clear to the back of parking lot. Everyone thought it was hysterical. Well, except one person.

The groom-to-be, right?

Wrong.

In fact, it was the clown who had the frown. Apparently he felt a little misled about the nature of this assignment. On top of that, he apparently was a little sensitive by nature, and was already having a bad few days. And he most certainly was not used to being laughed at by adults (or whatever this group of guys could be considered). The clown suddenly realized that he was in a bar, in costume, being heckled.

He not-so-politely excused himself and went to the front bar, where he began drinking in hopes of forgetting the whole ordeal.

And that, kids, is how a clown became a drunken angry clown. The violence? Well, that comes next. We are about to place you into this fracas, and your first move is to try to apologize. Good luck with that. Get ready to self-defend, because apparently drunken angry clowns don't accept apologies.

Setting the Scene: Who is This Clown?

Make all the jokes you like about Pennywise from "*It.*" The fact is, clowns are supposed to be fun. Unless you suffer from Coulrophobia (fear of clowns), you should find them likeable. Or at least more likeable than, say, a mime. They are supposed to enjoy leading the laughs and being the star of a fun event.

But sometimes something weird happens on the way to fun. Sometimes your attempts at fun lead to jokes and pranks. Sometimes those jokes and pranks cross the line. And sometimes you encounter a drunken, angry clown in a bar.

OK, that last one probably doesn't happen as often as "sometimes." In fact, if it has ever happened more than once, you may want to talk to someone.

But here you are, fresh from what you thought was a fun prank. Hire a clown instead of a stripper. Add him to a bachelor party. Watch the fun. Except your contracted clown didn't cooperate. He chose instead to pout over the lack of respect you demonstrated for his comedic profession. Instead of playing along, he is now taking advantage of the venue to drink all of his problems away.

Your Bar-jutsu training calls for polite management of potentially confrontational situations. So you give your funny friend time to cool off and then approach him to ask forgiveness. Let's just say that his reaction is very un-clown like. Instead of extending an olive branch, he downs his double-martini with extra olives and then attacks you.

This puts you somewhere that you never ever thought you would be. You are in a bar, about to defend yourself against an attack from a circus clown. When this is done, you may very well need therapy.

Introduction to the Maneuver: Who Is This Clown?

1. Here's something you don't read every day: a circus clown is about to hit you. As his right arm extends out you step slightly back and to the outside of his right hand with your left leg.

2. Bring your left hand over the top of his right hand and bring your right hand up and grab the side of his fist where his pinky finger is. When you have a firm grip with both of your hands slide your left foot back past your right leg then slide your right foot up, maintaining your balance. When you shift your body, make sure that you torque his fist back so that his knuckles bend back across his forearm.

3. When he drops to the ground, keep control of the clown until he realizes that he made a mistake and it wasn't just the choice of profession. Do not bend with him, this will cause you to lose balance and allow him to pull you over. If needed, bend at the knees and squat down keeping your back straight. If he continues to fight, place your knee behind his elbow, apply pressure and turn him over onto his belly.

PRACTICING THE MANEUVER:

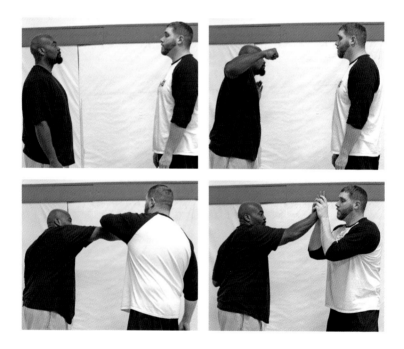

1. Both partners stand just outside of arm's length away.

2. Attacker throws a right punch aiming for defender's face.

3. Defender steps just to the outside of the punch, bringing your left hand over top of the punching right hand.

4. Defender brings his right hand up from underneath and grabs the inside of the punching palm. Defender slides left foot back and to the right, turning his body while gripping punching fist with both hands.

5. As your body turns, force the pinky knuckle on the punching fist back and across the forearm diagonally. The turning of the body will cause the fist to turn. Slide the left foot back and take attacker down to the ground.

6. Repeat steps for both right and left sides.

Lesson 10:
BEING THE BEST BAR-JUTSU

Can we let you in on a little secret?

We hate cats.

OK, "hate" is a strong word. But we definitely don't trust them. Cats seem to be up to something. Something bigger than us. No one really knows what. World domination? Perhaps. Household domination? For sure. We believe that they have already formed some sort of global union and are plotting their next moves.

We'll give cats credit for one thing, however. The whole "nine lives" thing. You have to respect anything that can live eight lives and still have something left in the tank. Can you imagine all that you could do with nine lives?

In effect, you have done just this—you are not so different from cats in this regard.

You have just completed nine lessons. In effect you have lived nine lives. You've been touched, and you've touched. You fought off an accuser who swears you stole his dog. You've had your back against the wall, you've dodged broken glass, and you've even fought off crazed fans as a rock star. You've acted a drunken clown, and fought a drunken clown.

You've lived a full life. Nine times.

And now, you get to go where no cat has gone before. Life number ten.

In this lesson, we would like to take you on a tour of your past lives. No worries…we're not going to send you ghosts of Bar-jutsu past, present, and future to show you how different the world would have been without your Ebenezer Scrooge self. We already know what joy you've brought to the world. For one, you've purchased our book.

Instead, we'd simply like to add some tips that apply to Lessons 1-9, and illuminate a few things that may not have been so obvious to you at the time. After all, we want you to make us proud should you ever have to defend yourself. You're Bar-jutsu family now. We want to brag. We'd rather you not become the weird uncle we never talk about.

If Practice Does Not Make Perfect, Practice and Practice Again

No doubt you've heard all the clichés:

- *Practice makes perfect.*
- *If at first you don't succeed, try and try again.*
- *He who hesitates to practice is like a rolling stone that gathers no moss but does gather bruises and needs nine stitches in time.*

OK, so not all of the above are real clichés. But what makes a cliché real anyway? The point is, in order to be effective with something, effort is needed. In the case of self-defense, that effort means practice.

It is our belief that the instructions in the book, coupled with the images, should prove helpful to you in learning the maneuvers. You should be able to break down each maneuver, step-by-step, and try it yourself. Slowly at first. With a partner. As you feel more comfortable, you can shake things up a bit. Increase the speed. Practice right-handed and left-handed. Practice being the defender, and the aggressor. See how the other half lives. You'll be amazed at what you learn about defending if you fight in the shoes of the attacker. Just don't keep them.

A big part of self-defense is instinct. Instinct doesn't necessarily mean natural instinct. With enough practice, you can make a maneuver something that is instinctive to you.

Bar-jutsu says: Self-defense is most effective when the moves become instinctive. Instincts are not necessarily natural; they can be developed through repetition and practice.

We're not even going to bring up the example of the Karate Kid movies, where a young boy developed karate instincts by repeatedly waxing a car and painting a fence. No way, not even going to mention it. Not in this book. That would be way too cliché. However, if you don't agree to practice your maneuvers, we may just have you start doing a few chores around the Bar-jutsu headquarters.

As this final lesson is more of a review with additional tips, we will spare you the scenario. You've already had nine lives anyway. Now that you're in "overtime," so to speak, we just want you to be yourself. And we want you to be the best that Bar-jutsu has to offer.

Preparing for Practice

1. When practicing any technique, it is important to take care of your partner. Allow him to roll with each throw and to bend with each move.

2. Stretch before you train.

3. In reality, you might have to add a punch, kick, or even head-butt to truly get the desired result. Never go at full speed while training. The goal is to learn the maneuver without causing serious injury to you or your training partner. Train smart.

4. When we train at the Bar-jutsu Dojo, we wear traditional uniforms or comfortable street clothes for a realistic affect (since it's not often you walk into a bar wearing a ninja uniform). Simulating reality is important. Try wearing different clothing that you are most likely to be wearing while out. Hats are fine, and can even prove helpful. If needed, a hat can be thrown into the face of an

opponent. It blinds or distracts just long enough for you to apply almost any move in this book.

Lesson 2: First Contact: Hey! He Touched Me

1. In Lesson 2, you learned the basic form of the technique and hopefully practiced it with a training partner. Once you have mastered the move, try adding this little bonus to make the technique more effective: as you step back and bring your arm across to grab, try an open-hand slap to the face. This will distract the attacker and make the technique much easier to apply. A good strike will really shake an opponent up a bit. Remember when practicing to keep it mild.

Lesson 3: First Contact: Oops! I Touched Him

1. In Lesson 3, as you destroy the balance of your attacker, slightly pull him in and drive the top of your head into his face.

2. Make sure you are striking with the hard part, which is just above the forehead and not top dead center of your dome.

3. Now that you've given your attacker a serious facial, their eyes will be tearing up and you can slide in and step on the back of the knee, forcing it down.

Lesson 4: Have You Got the Time?

1. In Lesson 4, again stepping back and destroying the balance, drive a punch into their stomach.

2. Once this unexpected strike is delivered, you can turn and punch through the elbow and complete the technique.

3. We actually prefer to backhand the rib cage. That is a target nearly guaranteed to drop an opponent.

4. Remember to use proper footwork and take out their legs to get them to the ground.

Lesson 5: Up Against the Wall

1. In Lesson 5, try using your knuckles and strike the outsides of the elbows instead of crashing down on top of them. Then you can use a head-butt to throw your opponent off of his game.

2. Keep in mind that in these combative situations, your fists are not your only tools to work with. Try using every part of your body to distract them.

Lesson 6: Is That a Broken Beer Bottle in Your Hand, Or Are You Just Happy to See Me?

1. In the scenario presented in Lesson 6, you may find yourself in a situation where you can't step inside the swing. That's ok. You still want to place yourself between the attacker and the weapon.

2. Step in just after the swing and trap his arm against your chest. Lock his elbow into a straight position and grab his wrist on the same hand. Use your other hand to blind him and push your chest out to apply pressure to the back of his elbow. This will cause him to lose him grip.

3. We hope this goes without saying, but when practicing this maneuver **please use a prop**! Like a plastic bottle. Or a foam football. Or a fruitcake.

Lesson 7: Karaoke-jutsu

1. The maneuver in Lesson 7 can be enhanced with a step. A simple step or kick to the back of the knee will drop your opponent much faster and take his attention away from his arm being entangled.

Lesson 8: I'm Not As Think As You Drunk I Am

1. In Lesson 8, when the punch is thrown, start out the same way but turn your body so that your right side is now against his right side. Allow his arm to drape across your chest as your left hand is now grabbing his right wrist. Step your right foot directly behind his right foot and open your right hand up into his face. A simple twist of your upper body and a little force to his face will send him backwards. Maintain control throughout the technique and if needed lock his elbow against your knee.

Lesson 9: Who Is This Clown?

1. Insist that your partner dress like a clown. It probably won't work, but of it does please send your photos to james@barjutsu.com or post them to our Facebook page at http://www.facebook.com/Bar-jutsu123.

2. As the clown punch comes in and you slip to the outside, deliver a swift and meaningful kick to his midsection. This distraction will knock the wind out of him and make this technique much easier to apply.

LAST CALL

Congratulations! You have completed your Bar-jutsu training. Where did the time go? It seems like just yesterday, we were meeting each other in that bookstore. And now, after all the lessons and bad jokes we've shared with you, we're headed for some dusty bookshelf. Or maybe you're sending us to your friend's house, since he's too cheap to buy the book himself.

We hope that you have something better in mind for us. When you bought *Bar-jutsu: The American Art of Bar Fighting*, you became more than a book sale to us. We'd like to think that you became part of the Bar-jutsu family. Family means something to us. The Bar-jutsu movement is not about drinking or violence. It is all about having fun and staying safe. It's about preserving all that is good about bars and pubs. It's about camaraderie. And you can't have camaraderie without comrades (we checked; you need one to have the other). To us, camaraderie means *family*. So welcome to the family!

We look out for family. So we hope the lessons in this book help to defend you and yours should your good times meet someone who fell off the family tree. Hopefully, you'll re-read the lessons in this book. More importantly, we hope that you'll review the maneuvers. Unless you plan on throwing this book at an attacker, it does no good to you without practicing the contents. Practice the maneuvers. Practice the principles we've preached. Stay in control. Be a defender, not an attacker. Keep a sense of humor. That's how the Bar-jutsu family rolls.

Parting is such sweet sorrow. Actually, we've never really understood what that means. But we do know that there never seems to be enough time to say everything you want to say. On the other hand…it's our book. So before we reach the end, here are a few "Last Call" thoughts:

Last Call #1: Drink Up. But Know When to Stop.

We've cracked a great deal of jokes in this book about drinking. When you have seen as many people get drunk as we have, it's hard not to laugh. It helps keeps us sane. But excessive drinking is no laughing matter. Recall again everything Bar-jutsu stands for. Does getting sick in the parking lot or getting arrested for relieving yourself on a fire hydrant sound like staying in control?

Which brings us to the next thought…

Last Call #2: Drink Up. Just Don't Drive.

We understand how it starts. You're at a party. You're in a bar. Maybe you're hanging out with a group of friends. Or you've stopped for a happy hour drink after work. Whatever the reasons, you drive to a place where alcohol is pouring. And when you're done, you drive home.

Despite massive advertising campaigns, educational programs, and increasingly strict laws, drunk driving remains a reality. We won't even try to crack a joke about it. We've seen the horrors first-hand. We've seen people leave bars and never come back. We've seen good people who "only had a minor buzz going" climb into their car and forever destroy someone else's family. We know first-hand what a car can do to a body that cannot control it.

If you don't value your own life and well-being, then at least consider that of others. Yes, it's an inconvenience to you. Your car is already in the parking lot. How will you get back here to get it tomorrow? You only live 10 minutes away. Who are you going to call at this hour? Cabs are expensive.

Any idea how stupid these lines sound to a person who is lying in a hospital bed because of you?

Call it driving impaired. Call it drunk driving. Call it what you will. Just don't do it. We're counting on you. Make us proud.

Last Call #3: Don't Fight

We said it once (actually we said it more than one), we'll say it again. Fighting is stupid. It's the anti-fun. Defend yourself whenever needed. But never fight. Never attack. You can almost always defend yourself without coming to blows. If you find yourself repeatedly striking your opponent, you just may be fighting. Recall the courtroom scene that opened Lesson 3. If you had to recant your story to a judge (or a police officer, or your mother) would it sound as flimsy as that?

Last Call #4: Respect the Bar

Most bars and pubs are owned and managed by good people. Bartenders, table servers, and kitchen workers are hard-working people who are there to help your evening be a good time. Show them some respect. Show them some love (hitting on your waitress is not exactly what we mean). Tell them how much you appreciate them. Never tear the place up (unless you've been fending off attackers). Most of these establishments want to be great hosts. Be a good guest.

———

Again, welcome to the Bar-jutsu family. Not to sound like your grandmother, but we hope you don't forget about us. Please visit us often, at www.barjutsu.com, and like us on Facebook at www.facebook.com/Barjutsu123. We'd love to share some tips and updates with you. Even better, we'd love to have you send us stories and photos.

Finally, we'd like you meet some of the family. These are the folks that spent time hamming it up for the camera to help illustrate the points of the lessons.

The *Bar-jutsu Players* spent many weekends during the development of this book posing for cameras in bars, wrestling each other, throwing punches, and otherwise clowning around. Come to think of it, they do that every weekend anyway. Still, we love them like brothers and want them on our side if things ever start hitting the fan.

The *Bar-jutsu Girls* are more than just pretty faces. They're intelligent, funny, and great ambassadors of the Bar-jutsu approach. You may even see them some evening at bar near you. But don't get any ideas. We're very protective. Not that they need it; they know how to handle themselves. Besides, they're family, remember?

Here are some pictures from the family album. Enjoy!

ACKNOWLEDGMENTS

We would like to thank the following for their contributions to this book. None of this would have been possible (or nearly as much fun) without you. We consider you part of the Bar-jutsu family, and are forever indebted to you: David Bissel, Morgan Bohart, Kirsten Douglas, Bryan Caruso, Kailin Clawson, Michelle Cooper, Andrea Donohoe, Dan Carpenter, Amy Gorman & Gorman's Pub, Kevin Grodz, Brian Fischer, Leo Hughes & Brookline Pub, Jaymie Zerabell Greives, Danielle Gillner, Justin Idol, Kevin Kleinrock, Kevin Lobodinsky, Brandon Kurta, Lou Manolios & Getaway Café, Andrew Marsh, Shihan Ed Martin, Jesse Mellor, Anthony Mihelcic, Paul Morris, Steve McCall, William Notte, Michael Porco, David Prosperino, Chrystin Rice, Michael "Blade" Runco, Cameron Sczerba, Wyatt Sheer, Anthony Slaughter, Heather Stempler, Lauren Tangel, Vincent Valerio, Allie Zurawsky.

The Tuttle Story: "Books to Span the East and West"

Many people are surprised when they learn that the world's largest publisher of books on Asia had its humble beginnings in the tiny American state of Vermont. The company's founder, Charles Tuttle, came from a New England family steeped in publishing.

Tuttle's father was a noted antiquarian dealer in Rutland, Vermont. Young Charles honed his knowledge of the trade working in the family bookstore, and later in the rare books section of Columbia University Library. His passion for beautiful books—old and new—never wavered throughout his long career as a bookseller and publisher.

After graduating from Harvard, Tuttle enlisted in the military and in 1945 was sent to Tokyo to work on General Douglas MacArthur's staff. He was tasked with helping to revive the Japanese publishing industry, which had been utterly devastated by the war. After his tour of duty was completed, he left the military, married a talented and beautiful singer, Reiko Chiba, and in 1948 began several successful business ventures.

To his astonishment, Tuttle discovered that postwar Tokyo was actually a book-lover's paradise. He befriended dealers in the Kanda district and began supplying rare Japanese editions to American libraries. He also imported American books to sell to the thousands of GIs stationed in Japan. By 1949, Tuttle's business was thriving, and he opened Tokyo's very first English-language bookstore in the Takashimaya Department Store in Ginza, to great success. Two years later, he began publishing books to fulfill the growing interest of foreigners in all things Asian.

Though a westerner, Tuttle was hugely instrumental in bringing a knowledge of Japan and Asia to a world hungry for information about the East. By the time of his death in 1993, he had published over 6,000 books on Asian culture, history and art—a legacy honored by Emperor Hirohito in 1983 with the "Order of the Sacred Treasure," the highest honor Japan can bestow upon a non-Japanese.

The Tuttle company today maintains an active backlist of some 1,500 titles, many of which have been continuously in print since the 1950s and 1960s—a great testament to Charles Tuttle's skill as a publisher. More than 60 years after its founding, Tuttle Publishing is more active today than at any time in its history, still inspired by Charles Tuttle's core mission—to publish fine books to span the East and West and provide a greater understanding of each.